Remember When

Doris Schroeder

Doris Schroeder

Copyright © 2008 Doris Schroeder

Author Edited

Cover: Richard Henry

ISBN 978-09815522-3-4

1110 West 5th Street
Coffeyville, Kansas, 67337

Printed in the United States of America

Dedication

On a lonely Kansas hill, located by a shelterbelt of old trees and a barbed wire fence, sits the place that once fanned my imagination into the field of writing. Strange to say, it was located on a country thoroughfare now named Sunrise Road.

Even now, the crows that croon are voicing the same lullaby of by-gone days and the melancholy melody of the Kansas farm that once existed. The rays of the prairie sunrise from the east used to dance through all the long, lean windows of the old two story farmhouse in which we lived, fueling my little girl's imagination with a burning desire to pencil my observations onto my Big Chief pencil tablet.

H.G. Wells penned these words in 1901: "The past is but the beginning of a beginning, and all that is and has been is but the twilight of the dawn." In other words, no matter what happens in this life, we can know and be certain that "sunrise always comes!"

Sunrise on the farm always gave me a thrill. Shortly before the sun's grand entrance, the rooster would announce her coming like the trumpet for the king. Sometimes this would cause a brief scurry of the barn yard cats as they began their vigil of watching the front door. Even our two farm dogs, Shep and Spot, began their observation, knowing that soon, with the coming of their caretaker, they would be fed their morning repast. Occasionally you could hear the plaintive groan of a cow, impatiently waiting to be milked.

And then it came! Just a hint of a promise at first, brief streaks of color in the drab gray sky, then a little more, and suddenly the sunrise broke out and washed the landscape in a kaleidoscope of vibrant colors and the world became alive, a new day had arrived!

And it kept coming...to my great-grandparents who had come from Russia to build this farm, to my grandparents who had continued farming with horses, and finally to my dad, who farmed with tractors and me, a gangly farm girl.

As the writer of this piece, I have grown up with a deep love for America and for the state of Kansas. The God my ancestors worshipped has become my God when I accepted him into my life. He is the God who watches over us and our family now.

The hill where our farmhouse had weathered the storms of Kansas is now bare. All the buildings have been moved away: the big red barn with the hayloft, the windmill that could sound like a Kansas melody on a windy day, the big yellow, two story farmhouse in which I had learned to write words in my big chief pencil tablet, the long driveway to the road with the Russian mulberry trees planted by the side...all gone now, with nothing left but the green wheat sparkling in the Kansas sun like an emerald sea of promise!

The promise of freedom to my ancestors who came for the freedoms of America and dared to do something that they had never done before. The promise that beckons to everyone that believes in God...

I still drive by this area from time to time and thank God that my ancestors did come to America. It is through all of this, I can now say with deep conviction: "I am a Christian and I am an American!"

I dedicate these memories to each of you who remember a simpler time in history. A time that we address now as "Remember When...!"

Doris Schroeder

Acknowledgements

Without the help of my wonderful husband, there would have been no way to get my writing done. He stands by to help with household chores of a retired couples' home. He helps with the meals, vacuuming the carpet, and simply being there as I get my deadlines done. I couldn't do it without him.

There are many people along the way that encourage a writer. Being a member of the Kansas Authors Club has helped a lot. Of course, during my three year presidency, there wasn't a lot of extra time, but getting to know the other writers and working with them has taught me a lot about "hanging in" when the going gets rough. As a board, we have learned to stay the course when the good and bad times come. This is so true in writing. If it's a dream you want to achieve, you have to stick it out, no matter what comes!

The state writing contest helped, especially when the judges gave a critique with each entry. That is what it is all about. Even our local writer's group is helpful, when we hear others read what they have written and look for ways to better themselves and their writing. There are so many friends in both groups; I hesitate to mention them for fear of leaving some out. I do thank all of you!

We have 5 grandsons: John Edward, Jesse, Ryan, Jason and Michael, and each one has been very special in my life. When they were younger, they often spent the night with Grandma and Grandpa, and listened eagerly to my stories about my childhood. They also gave me a lot to write about in my columns. This was a great encouragement. Every one of them have a bit of a writer in them, if they ever want to pursue it.

In earlier years, I contemplated the computer but couldn't get up the nerve to learn it. Our youngest grandson, Mike, came over one day, carrying his old computer and said "Grandma, you are going to learn the computer, 'cause I'm going to teach you!" And he did! He got me past being scared of it and taught me all the new ways I could make posters and pamphlets. Above all, I found it much easier to write on than a typewriter.

Our own children John and Judy, who also have been a big part of our life. John has taken up some writing now as well, writing for the Kansas Senior times. Judy has more of the artistic qualities as she trains others as a physical trainer at the Hutchinson Y.

I appreciate all those who helped me find pictures for my book: my sister, Carol, my old friend, Ruth Witt, my cousin Lou Ediger and several others.

In earlier years, my teacher, Esther Willems, and in high school, Esther Pankratz. My creative writing teacher at HJCC, Steve Hinds, who didn't always agree with me, but helped me understand what I was saying when I wrote and he gave me a good grade at the end. They all gave me the encouragement I needed and I will always be grateful to them.

The Young at Heart Ministries, a local group who meet every Thursday morning at the Delos Smith Center, are a great encouragement to my writing. They share many of their memories with me. I love and appreciate each one of them.

The editors of the papers I write for have given me the chance and they are much appreciated: Mike Alfers, *The Rural Messenger*, Joe Sporleder, *the Kansas Senior Times*, and John Montgomery with *The Hutchinson News*.

Above all, I thank God for never giving up on me. Sometimes, I think it is a wonder He doesn't throw up his hands and say "That's it!" He made it a passion of mine, giving me encouragement when I needed it and peace when it got too much. I know He is my greatest friend and confidant! All my life, I wondered what He really wanted me to do, and it seems that writing is IT!

Doris Schroeder

Table of Contents

Page

Chapter 1

Life moved at a slower pace!

The house where we lived on W. 14th

Life is changing at a much faster rate than we can comprehend. You go to bed one night and by morning, you are out of style! There are many things that have changed for the better but there are a number of simpler truths that need to remain!

One of the first memories I had as a little girl of three and a half, was that of the friendly neighborhood in the 300 block of West 14th, in Hutchinson, Kansas. Life was simple for our little family of four. We lived in a rented bungalow house. I had an almost six-year-old sister, my mom and dad, and life was pretty much uncomplicated.

My dad went to work every day: mom took care of the house and us two little girls. Each day we walked to the grocery store, which was located on Main Street between 13th and 14th. Life was grand, and slow.

There weren't many cars screeching down the street because not everyone owned a car, no, not even one. Sometimes, if one of the neighbors was going to town they would ask if anyone wanted a ride. Most of the time, however, if mom wanted to go downtown to pay utility bills, she would take Luella and me along and we walked, all 24 blocks to town. My sister and I skipped along the sidewalks, careful not to step on the cracks. We remembered the old adage "Step on a crack and break your mother's back!" Of course, not having TV at that time, we did not even imagine such a cruelty as that!

For some reason, we did not have a refrigerator. We had an old ice box in the kitchen, which is probably why mom walked to the store every day. At certain times, mom would put the card in the window; it either had a big 25 or 50 number stamped on it. Luella and I could hardly wait for the ice truck to drive slowly by our house. If our card was up, the ice man would stop and if we asked politely, gave us a sliver of ice to lick. Then he took his tongs and carried the ice to the back door. The ice was heavenly!

In the evening hours, when the air was just a bit cooler, our parents would sit on our front porch, a flyswatter in their hand to slap the mosquitoes and flies, and visit back and forth with the neighbors across the way. We children played the fun games of hide and go seek and different kinds of tag. We thought we had it made.

No one had a lot of worldly goods, so there was little talk of wealth or influence. People in our neighborhood were pretty much on the same level. That was probably the reason there was a lot of sharing. If one mother baked cookies one day, many of us children shared in their consumption. If something exciting happened at one family's house, like a cat having kittens, we all got to enjoy the event. Few people had telephones so we just called out to the neighbors.

My mother had her daily chores: wash on Monday, iron on Tuesday, bake on Wednesday and Saturday, clean on Friday, and church on Sunday. As long as that was accomplished each day, she knew she was on target.

My greatest enjoyment was getting mom to tell us stories about when she was young. She was an expressive storyteller and we took great pleasure in hearing about her life in younger years, how she tipped over the Model T by turning too sharp, how one of their students in the country school where they both taught, put a skunk in dad's desk drawer, and things like that.

Sometimes she went to the neighbors and helped quilt. That was a treat for us kids. The mothers would always bring home-baked goodies, made from scratch, naturally, and of course, we kids got to enjoy them.

Life was moving at a slower pace and everyone enjoyed the simple things they had. I wish we could slow down the business of today's life. If we would at least take an hour each day to enjoy the moment! We could use the minds God gave us to meditate and enjoy life with the people around us.

Chapter 2

I faced my first tragedy

My sister, Luella Grace Kroeker,
in the casket after the shooting

It was August, 1936, and it was hot.

The New-Herald reported the temperature and it was the highest reported in Kansas for a long time. In fact, my dad had read to me from the paper the night before that "it was so hot, you could fry an egg on the side walk!"

I remember thinking "How could you scrape it up?"

Since I was only three and a half at that time, I didn't mind the heat. My almost six-year-old sister, Luella, had just graduated from Roosevelt Kindergarten that spring and I could trust her to keep me entertained.

On this particular day, we had made mud pies in our playhouse in back of the garage. It was so much fun to mix the black dirt with a coffee can of water that we got from the outside spigot. We'd mix it, just like mom did, and then we poured the concoction into coffee can lids and let them bake in the hot Kansas sun.

I was surveying the results of my efforts when suddenly Lulu stopped and asked "Do you hear that?"

I shook my blond, bobbed hair negatively, "I don't hear nothing!"

"I think I hear some kittens across the street! Let's go over and see them!"

Cats weren't my favorite animals but anything Lulu wanted to do was fine with me. "Okay!" I agreed.

We ran into the house to ask permission from our mom. She was ironing at the dining room table and I could see little drops of sweat on her forehead. She smiled at our excited question and gave us permission to go across the street with special directions to Lulu "Be sure and take hold of Doris' hand when you cross the street and come home when you see dad's car home for supper!"

We nodded our heads affirmatively and ran across the street. Soon Luella was playing with the little balls of fur and cooing to them like a mother cat. Other neighbor kids were there also, some played jacks and everyone was having a good time.

I was a little impatient and soon was looking out of the front room window, wondering when my dad would come home. As I watched, the neighbor's father came home, parking by the curb. He stopped to talk to another neighbor. His little boy, the same age as my sister, ran out to ask if he could carry in his hunting gun. Not thinking it was loaded, he handed it to his son, Billie. I could tell he was thrilled that his dad trusted him to carry it in.

I watched as he came in the house. He pretended he was playing Cowboys and Indians, like in the movies, and pointed it at Lulu and pulled the trigger. She fell to the floor with a large red spot on her polka-dotted dress. His mom came running in from the kitchen and then she, too, fell over.

"Something's not okay!" I thought and ran out of the house, down the steps and across the street, to tell my mom. She was coming at a run because she, too, had heard the shot through the open windows.

Other people of our friendly neighborhood came dashing out, too. When one man saw what had happened, he ran to his garage and backed out his car. Mom jumped in the back seat and they handed Lulu to her and they took out...fast.

I think I started to cry. "Something was certainly not right!" I wasn't sure what it was but I knew I didn't like it. One of the neighbors, Mrs. Smith, took me over to her house until my Aunt Martha came and got me and took me to their house on West 11th.

All evening, no one talked much and everyone looked so sad. My cousins, Della and Lou, were quiet and I couldn't quite figure out why.

It had been dark a long time when my gray faced father came to pick me up. He did not smile like he usually did and when I asked where Lulu was, he told me she had gone to heaven.

That puzzled me. "Why didn't she take me along?" I wondered and even felt a little mad that she didn't tell me she was leaving. I also wondered if heaven was a real place or make believe like some of the fairy tale stories. I made up my mind to find out, no matter how long it took.

The headlines of the Hutchinson News-Herald the next day said something about "A friendly neighborhood turns sad because of an accidental shooting."

Like most of you, I had experienced my first life tragedy and I, too, was sad! But life did what it always does, it went on, even in spite of tragedy. And my life's quest started out to find out if there really is a heaven.

Chapter 3

Running away from home for ice cream

**My cousin, Della, and me playing by my house,
after our ice cream cones**

The dog days of summer are beginning to tease our dispositions again, and sometimes it is hard to keep a smile on our face. In my estimation there are two words, however, that can defuse the hottest element of my disposition...ice cream!

Personally, those words can paint such a picture in my mind, I can almost drool at the very thought of such a cooling concoction, just ask my husband, John!

Do you remember when this treat was not so easy to come by? When we had ice boxes in our kitchen and no automatic refrigerators, we could not keep this cool stuff cold, leave alone have enough grocery money to buy it.

This time the year was 1937, a year later than last year. A lot had happened since the year before. my older sister, Luella, had been accidentally shot and killed by a neighbor boy and I was now an only child. I was 4 1/2, and felt more of a compulsion to check things out on my own.

It was exciting to sit on my mother's lap as my dad drove our Model A down the brick main streets of Hutchinson. One hot summer day, I listened carefully as my parents discussed this new store on the corner of 5th & main. If I remember correctly, it was called the Peter Pan Ice Cream Store and it served something I was not yet acquainted with, ice cream cones.

Dad parked in the space next to the store on 5th Avenue and I watched the people going in and out. many came out with a cone shaped cookie topped by a round scoop of ice cream. I wanted one in the worst way!

"Now, Doris, you stay here with dad and I'll be right back!" Mom promised. When she came back out, she was carrying three dripping ice cream cones and she carefully handed one to me. I observed how she and dad licked the cool ambrosia and I tried to do the same. "Good!" was my instant reaction and I enjoyed every last lick.

In fact, as we chugged down Main Street to our home on West 14th, a little plan began to evolve in my mind. "I want another one!" was the thought I was entertaining. "As soon as we get home, I'll tell my mom and dad I want to play in my playhouse in back of the garage. Instead, I'll walk back to the store and get another ice cream cone!" Of course, the fact that I needed a nickel to buy it, escaped my thinking completely!

As we drove home, I tried to remember the way. I needed to get to Main Street from the 300 block of West 14th. For some reason, I overshot Main and landed on East 14th Street.

"This doesn't look quite right!" I decided and strolled back to Main. I turned south at the corner and then ambled on past 13th and then 12th Street, hoping I was on the right track. I was beginning to wonder if I had done the right thing. I hoped I wasn't lost!

I felt the first pangs of panic and began to wish I hadn't been so daring. I heard a car chug up to the curb. "It's dad!" I thought gratefully. I ran to the car door just as he opened it and I crawled in. Dad didn't say a word as we silently drove to our house. By then, I didn't care if I got another cone or not, I was just plain glad to get home!

We discussed the situation when I got to the house and I tried to tell my parents why I had run away from home. "I just needed another ice cream cone!" I was grateful they understood and the only "licking" I got was the next time they stopped at the Peter Pan Store!

I do, by the way, still love ice cream but I don't have to run away to get some. We have some in the freezer! Isn't God good to us? He gives us more than we want or need. However...!

Chapter 4

The 4th of July

My cousins from my mother's side, the Langes,
at the 4th of July celebration:
Back: Paul and Louie Lange, Jim Winter
Front: Johnnie & Dickie Winter, Doris Kroeker, Jerome &
Dorothy Lange

Freedom means different things to different people. Sometimes we forget to thank God for the fact that we are living in America, enjoying many more freedoms than we deserve. We forget the sacrifice of the men who signed the Declaration of Independence in 1776, the soldiers who have given their life to keep these freedoms alive and our ancestors who, with great courage, moved their families to the United States of America, so we, too, could enjoy life in the best sense of the word. Too often, we take our freedom to worship God for granted.

My first Fourth of July began as a hot, muggy July day. The calendar on the wall at my grandparents' house in Buhler had the year 1937 on it. The flies swarmed around the screen door of "Little" Grandma's house. The chatter of my cousins was audible through the open door, so I ran ahead of my parents, throwing open the door with such abandonment that some of the pests infiltrated the house.

My Uncle Herb was soon standing by the door, swishing a fly swatter right and left, mumbling something about "kids these days!"

Of course I did not recognize my part in the fiasco, and ran into the middle bedroom where my young relatives were draped around the bed, talking.

"Did you bring any firecrackers?" my cousin Dickie asked. "We get to do fireworks tonight!"

My blond, bobbed hair shook negatively. My four-year-old mind was pleased that my older cousin would even think me capable of lighting a firecracker. "If he just knew how scared I am of those things!" I thought. "But I'll never let him know!"

Even the little town of Buhler was exciting on a holiday. Life was still simple and nice and uncomplicated. Kind of like leftover mashed potatoes when you're really hungry.

Talking ceased momentarily as my grandfather stood at the doorway, glaring at us. He had a certain look about him, due to his bad eyesight, that always made me speechless. He was a commanding figure who worked as a miller at the Dixie Lily Flour Mill in Buhler.

Grandpa must have experienced an exciting life, moving his family from Germany to Russia to escape the militarism of that day. Then to move them to the United States took a lot of gumption. My mom was even born on the ship coming over.

He didn't talk much, at least that I remember. That was probably because he could only speak German. I was always in awe of him, as were my other cousins. That is, all of them except Dickie. He'd always say something a little smart-alecky to him and I trembled at his audacity.

Soon, Little Grandma was bustling around, putting supper on the big dining room table. She was so little but so mighty, always serving people and dashing around as a dynamo of energy, entirely inconsistent with her petite frame. Family dinners were huge platters of food, elegantly served on a white tablecloth; good china and the Jell-O served in exquisite champagne glasses and topped with real whipping cream.

Later, all the grown ups sat outside on dining room chairs. As dusk began to fall, Main Street became an extravaganza of staccato sounds, pop, pop, pop.

That was the year I was introduced to the sparkler. At first I was sure the shooting sparks would certainly burn up my hand, but not wishing cousin Dickie to know of my fear, I gingerly picked one up and swished it around a few times. When I found out the sparks didn't hurt one bit, I was fascinated with the designs I could make in the sky.

Soon my cousin Dorothy and I were artists of the night sky, swirling every design we could imagine. We were overjoyed with this new invention. It was hard to contain our amazement.

When the supply of sparklers diminished, I crawled up on my dad's lap and watched the neighbor kids down the block light up some special fireworks. There was no traffic down the main street of Buhler that night as people sat out in the warm night air.

Some of my uncles turned the crank on the ice cream freezer by the back porch and we were all brought whopping dishes of homemade ice cream, along with some crackers to "take away the sweet taste."

The stern silhouette of my Grandfather Lange against the summer night sky seemed fitting. We should celebrate our country's freedom with the relative who had the courage to move his family across the ocean to the "land of the free!" It also felt comforting to have family around after the accidental death of my sister the summer before.

God has been good to us and our country. Let's remember to thank him for all the freedoms we enjoy!

Chapter 5

Old time cooking

My mom could cook on anything

We have just had a new cook stove put in our kitchen and have so many gadgets to help us in our culinary achievements. I should be able to be the food cook of the year, but I'm not! Oh, I have a lot of reasons why I'm not, stemming from lack of time to perhaps, a lack of passion for cooking up a storm. Although I can fix food adequately, I will never be famous for my cookery.

Such was not the case with my mom's cuisine in her earlier days. We moved around a lot and she could cook on a little two-burner or a nice four burner gas range. On the farm in the forties, she had a three-burner kerosene stove with a separate oven that had to be put on two kerosene burners in order to bake. In each scenario, the baked goods came out mouth-watering delicious.

When I got home from school, having walked the dusty country road or across the wheat field, I always ran the last few steps into the old farmhouse. I knew mom would be there most of the time, her apron tied around her print house dress and a little smile on her face. Waiting on the oilcloth covered farm table was the baked or cooked delicacy of the day, painstakingly made on the old kerosene stove. Sometimes it was chocolate cupcakes, cream puffs or chocolate pudding, but always delicious. All of this was made from scratch, as mixes were not even in the cooking vocabulary of the day. No, you younger cooks, you could not buy scratch at the grocery store!

Pudding for the cream puffs or just to eat was made in a double boiler and took quite some time on the kerosene stove. Sometimes it was my job to keep stirring the mixture with the water boiling below, so it would not burn.

"I don't think my mom will like that!" I told my cousin, Dick Winter, when he was at our house sometimes after mom had made one of her delicious chocolate cakes with creamy fudge frosting. He licked all the frosting off and told me it was because he couldn't stop, it was so good!

One family Christmas was held at our farm in the forties and I remember my mom making lots of fudge and storing it in oatmeal boxes. Actually, it was surprising the boxes made it until the gathering with all of us around. We did not "fudge" about our love for this stuff!

It is true that my mom was a good candy maker because she also liked fudge. In later years we took her along to Colorado on vacation and enjoyed looking at souvenirs in Manitou Springs. As we entered a candy shop, I told her she shouldn't buy more than one piece of fudge since too much wouldn't be good for her. Not to be outdone, she did buy just one piece, a whole half-pound portion!

She loved to bake either bread or zwie bach at least every other day. When she made the German, two-bun bread, she also made some into coffee cakes, sprinkling them with sugar and cinnamon. I knew when I tired of making mud pies, I could go in and have some real food.

When my girlfriend, Ruth, came over to play, mom would bake us something special. Ruth's mother, Mrs. Friesen, was the same way. If I visited Ruth while she was herding cows along the road, her mother would see us from a distance and would make her famous doughnuts or crullers and call us in later for "faspa," which was a German traditional, 4 o'clock lunch.

Her stove intrigued me because it was so much bigger than ours. It was large and black with a place to burn wood in it to make the fire hot for cooking or baking. It certainly heated up the house in summer but we didn't mind because of the treat it afforded us.

Sometimes my aunt and uncles would visit us during the week. I remember my Uncle George especially liked mom's Berlin cookies. These were made from dough similar to New Year's cookies but instead of raisins, a plum was inserted. This was fried in deep fat and sugared on the outside. Delicious!

Life was hard and earnest in the 40s. We really had to skimp and save. We did, however, have some things we do not have today. That consisted of putting in an honest day's work, enjoying the simple pastime of walking and talking to each other and having the time to converse and to listen to God. He was around, as he is today, but we could hear him better.

And mom's cooking was the best!

Chapter 6

Learning the lessons of life...alone

My dad's family get-together at the farm.
Back: Eddie, George and Mary Schierling, Emma Kroeder,
Martha Ediger, Ed Kroeker, John Ediger, Eldo Schmidt
Front: George Kroeker, Della Ediger, Dorothy Schierling,
Doris Kroeker, Grandma & Grandpa Kroeker,
Esther Schmidt

There had been some bad times and some good times in my life by the year 1937. I had enjoyed having an older sister, who had been accidentally shot and killed by a neighbor boy. Now, I was an only child. I was 4 years old and tried to reason out why things happened but couldn't always understand the whys and wherefores of life.

Now that I no longer had a big sister to protect me, I had to face some of the scarier things of life on my own. Before, Luella had always protected me from the neighbor boys, who liked to tease me. I can remember her shaking a stick at them and saying "You leave my little sister alone!" And they did!

After she was gone, they had a field day. Once they locked me in an outside shed. I tried to open the door but couldn't and I cried and cried. I don't remember who finally let me out.

I can remember my mom and dad taking me to the doctor in the Model T because the boys had hit me in the stomach with a tin can. I sure hoped they were sorry and would never do that again. They probably didn't because mom gave them a tongue lashing.

I do think, however, they finally got tired of teasing me. My mind recalls going to their homes and playing. They taught me some interesting new games like Tiddlywinks. Perhaps their mothers stepped in and made them be nice to me, because they finally were. I sure was glad that worry was over and life became more normal again.

When I saw the older girls walking home from school, I remember thinking to myself "Why do I always want to run and meet them?" I couldn't seem to help myself. They talked to me like big sisters, and I was always welcome in their homes.

The neighbors in the 300 block of West 14th were kind to me, whenever I would knock at their door, they would invite me in. I visited a new mother and her baby, watched her bathe the infant in this new contraption that folded up when it was not being used. It was called a baby bathinette, although I can no longer find that word in the dictionary.

A teacher named Woods and his wife lived on the corner. They also had a baby and a new invention called a refrigerator. One day, they made a concoction called sherbet and of course, invited me to have some. My mother had told me to come home by a certain time as Aunt Martha would soon be there to take us to Wednesday night church. I, however, thought, "I have to taste this sherbet thing because they said it was like ice cream!"

When I finally started home, I saw my aunt's car already backed out in the middle of the street, just about to leave without me. I couldn't believe it! How could they do such a thing? Needless to say, I learned my lesson on that one. The next time, I came right away!

We children met in the church basement together on Wednesday nights and when we were all together, we sang songs. There was one melody I wondered about. It was called "Climb, climb up Sunshine Mountain," and I tried to picture a mountain smiling. I wondered why I should climb it. I never did find out what it meant.

The kind neighbor lady next door to us always let me watch her wash her clothes on washday which, of course, was on a Monday. They had an outside cellar door that opened to their basement. She washed her clothes in a Maytag washer that they pulled outside. In summer, she had her rinse tubs outside in the backyard where she rinsed and wrung out the clothes before she hung them out on the line to dry. I loved to watch the whole process and probably asked a lot of questions as her work progressed.

One day, however, she was not in a good mood and she said to me "Why don't you go home, Doris, I don't have time for you today!"

This bothered me so much I ran home and hid in the closet, my secret hiding place. I couldn't understand why she was cranky at me. I tried not to be naughty!

I continued to learn the lessons of life that came my way, but it wasn't always easy. I wanted to know about whether heaven was a real place because that was where my sister was. Some of the grownups had said you have to be good to go there.

I tried to be good, but couldn't always do it. I hoped to find out the real answer some day!

Chapter 7

The best things in life are not free!

I know it is hard to believe as I opened my memory bank to my younger years, how much of that has stayed with me all this time. The earlier days' memories are part of my present day concepts, just as your memories have helped form you. In today's writing, I am still four years old.

My mother and I continued our daily walks to the grocery store, the icebox didn't keep meat very well so this was a usual occurrence. One day the clerk showed us some new cupcakes with a cream filling. "Mrs. Kroeker, wouldn't you and your little girl like to try these new cupcakes that are just out on the market? They are made by the Hostess Company and cost a nickel for a package of two. In fact, you can have a free package so you will know how good they taste."

"A free package of cupcakes!" That sounded great to me. As I thought about it, I surmised "Those chocolate cupcakes taste much better than my mud pies!" A plan began to form in my mind. "Why can't I just walk to the store each day and get a free package for my playhouse in back of the garage! What a great idea!"

This idea went on for a few days. Mom thought I was playing in back of the garage but instead I sneaked down the alley and walked to the grocery store. I picked up a package of the cakes and put them on the counter for the clerk to see, still thinking they were free. Later, I certainly enjoyed them when I had a tea party with my dolls. "They sure taste better than mud pies!" I told myself proudly, mentally patting myself on the back for being so clever.

One day, however, when mom and I had gone to the store, the clerk mentioned to my mother "Your little girl is sure charging a lot of cupcakes!" I was shocked as this knowledge was revealed.

"You mean they aren't free!" My mom just looked at me and smiled. When we got home, I hid in the closet. I was completely mortified. I didn't mean to have done wrong and I felt bad. My mother finally called me out and explained things to me.

It was back to making mud pies for me!

I kept trying to be what grownups called "good" but didn't always seem to make it. One Sunday, my dad, of all people, took me to the nursery where we sat with the babies. I tried to think what I had done wrong and couldn't remember why he took me there. I wanted to please him so much and I felt just terrible.

That night I dreamed we were in the church basement and they took the naughty kids in another room, one by one, but I couldn't see what was happening to them. Then it was my turn and I looked in the door. They were chopping off the heads of those who didn't behave. I woke up before they did mine. That dream stayed with me the rest of my life!

I kept trying. One evening the preacher and his family were over for supper. Later, their daughter, Bonnie Jean, and I were playing with sugar water by the kitchen table. I accidentally spilled mine on the floor. I told my mom that Bonnie Jean had done it. Then my conscience was so stricken: I hid again in the closet. My mom couldn't talk me out and neither could the preacher. I was so mad at myself. "Why can't I be good?" I fretted angrily.

I had heard the preacher at church tell us that if we did bad things, we would go to hell. I knew Luella was in heaven and I wanted to be sure that was where I was going, too, so I tried to be good. Somehow, and no matter how hard I tried, I couldn't quite make it. It seemed every once in awhile I did something naughty without really meaning to. I kept trying to find out how I could be certain of going to heaven someday but whenever I asked a grown up about it, they would smile and hand me a piece of gum or candy and pat me on the head. Even my Uncle Pete who was the preacher of the

Buhler MB Church did the same thing. I guess they thought I was too young to know about such things.

It was something I was going to find out, no matter what! I would also find out the best things in life, like chocolate cupcakes, are not free!

Chapter 8

Going to Kindergarten

The house on W. 9th St. where my friend, Anita, lived when we went to Allen Kindergarten. She later played "Helen Crump" on TV's Andy Griffith Show.

Many people have made the remark: "Everything I ever learned, I learned in kindergarten!" It is true we learn many of the basics of school when we attend kindergarten. It is a good thing, however, it doesn't end there!

Another year had passed and I was now a five-year-old. I couldn't say I now knew everything, but I sure was learning a lot about life. Our family moved away from our home on West 14th to a duplex on West 6th. It wasn't bigger, in fact, they had taken a regular house and made it into two living situations, so it really was only three rooms. I didn't care, life was good, I thought.

But now, the big moment was coming and I was about to begin my education. The kindergarten at Allen School was located in a white wooden building a block down from the big two-story stone building on Monroe Street.

The first day my mother walked me the six blocks to school from our house. I wondered what it would be like. Would I do well or would I make a complete fool of myself?

The teacher seemed to be a nice person. She told us where to sit and what we were going to learn this year. We sat at little tables and chairs. During a lull in the morning session, we were each given a little bottle of milk and a straw and a graham cracker. After we ate, we lined up to go to the restroom. I hated to stand in line because I felt like I was wasting time.

Finally, we were told to lay down on our little rug and try to sleep. The teacher played a hymn "Blest Be the Tie that Binds," while we rested our eyes. I liked that song and always felt peaceful when she played it. For some reason, it made me think of my sister, Luella, who had been accidentally shot and killed a couple years before. I have recently found out that my kindergarten teacher had also been my sister's teacher in 1936.

One day the teacher told us we were each going to get a shot. I had never had one before and was not eager about this situation. I decided I would try very hard not to cry. We walked in a line to the big school and into a classroom where a nurse was giving the injections. When it was my turn, I closed my eyes real tight and clamped my lips tight. I felt the jab, but I didn't cry. I sure wanted to, though!

I had many friends in kindergarten and I walked to school and back each day. If my mother was going to be gone, she stopped by the school and called me to the door. She would tell me who I was supposed to walk home with after school and sometimes I stayed at their house until a certain time.

One place I especially enjoyed going to was with my friend, Anita Courseau. She lived about two blocks from our house, on a beautiful tree-lined corner. I remember she seemed to be a very nice girl and she had a very cute outdoor playhouse that was so much fun to play in. Her mother wore high heels and earrings, even during the day and I was always impressed. It was many years later, I saw her play a TV role on Mayberry, playing the part of Helen Crump, the girlfriend of the sheriff. I have also found out she has passed on.

Another girl I stayed with lived in an upstairs apartment on Monroe. When I stayed with her, we had permission to have a bottle of pop out of their refrigerator. For some reason, I thought this was really living!

There was my friend Jane, who lived two houses down from us. We would play in her fenced in back yard. Our idols at that time were Hop A-Long Cassidy and Roy Rogers. Her father was a teacher at the college and on payday, would bring all his children little toys like balloons, color books, etc. I thought this was quite nice.

In the summer time, I decided to have a lemonade stand and my mother dutifully bought and made the lemon drink for me to sell. Most of my customers were the mailman, the iceman and a few passer bys. I made money but mom went in the hole, I'm sure.

When the weather got hot, the neighbor kids and I got an old wash tub, filled it with water, and took turns putting our head in it to see who could do it the longest. Actually, I wasn't too fond of that but certainly didn't want to appear chicken!

Life was continuing on and I was growing up. I still needed lots of answers to what life was all about but I felt confidant I would find the answers, in due time. God kept watching out for me in all my little endeavors as I grew up, at that time an only child.

Chapter 9

City girl moves to the country

Sunrise School, district 160

My learning years had started! After graduating from Allen Kindergarten in 1940, my dad and mom told me we were moving to the farm! Not only that but I could probably have a pony and learn to ride. That sure sounded exciting to me, then I could be a cowgirl and sing with Gene Autry and Roy Rogers!

However, this move would be a big adjustment. I had been in a city school and now would go to a one-room country school named Sunrise. This was the same school my father had attended in his earlier years. This was a whole new adventure!

I watched the countryside as we moved to the farm. My grandparents had lived there when my dad was little and now they had moved to Buhler, so I wanted to be sure to know the way. We drove past Medora, turned over the railroad tracks, curved around the river and kept going until we came to a country road (It is now named Sunrise Road). As we drove the half mile up the hill, I could hardly wait. The big yellow farmhouse and big red barn looked very inviting to a little six-year-old city girl who was about to make her debut into the first grade.

My mother bought me what I needed, a dinner bucket, a Big Chief Pencil Tablet and a pencil. On the first day she again walked me to school, approximately a little over a mile, to this grand experience.

The building was on the hill, a pert, white school that had stood so stalwartly through many years of educating the children of the district. I watched the dirt on the country road stretching up the hill that was to take me to this structure in all kinds of weather and different modes of transportation. At some places in the road, the trees made a canopy of greenery over my head as if to protect me from anything harmful that might come my way. I liked it.

When we got to the school, the children were playing outside on the merry go round and the swings. Mom introduced her and me to the teacher, Mr. Diener. Then she left and I was on my own. It was a little scary, but not too much.

Soon the teacher pulled the rope by the entrance and the big school bell changed us to attention. We lined up outside, marched in through the outside hall where the sink and hand pump were located, and went to our seats. I sat on the side with the little desks because there were only two other first graders, Ruth and Roland. the teacher said the pledge of allegiance and we all joined in. Even though I didn't know it, I liked the sound of it and it made me glad to be part of the United States. Then the teacher prayed and our day had begun.

As all eight grades concentrated on their lessons for the day, two old gentlemen peered down from their lofty picture on the wall, frowning in consternation when we made a mistake or used our time unwisely. I had a feeling, however, that if either Washington or Lincoln had been with us in person, they would have been pleased.

Mr. Diener told us the rules. If we had to go to the outhouse outside, we needed to raise one finger. If we wanted to sharpen our pencil, two fingers, and so on. Then he called the first grade to the front by saying "First Grade Reading." We got out our readers and went to the front.

As the days went by, the teacher taught us how to sound out words. One day, he was trying to get me to sound out the word h-u-g. For some reason, I tried and tried but couldn't quite get the word sounded out. Roland, the only boy in our class of three, laughed and said "You just don't want to say it!" I blushed when I came upon the answer. In those days, kids were not as out-spoken as they are today!

One day I noticed some of the older kids had things to say about the happenings of the world. I decided I had observed something quite unusual myself. I raised my hand and when the teacher called my name, I told him "When we were driving in Hutch, we drove by an alley and I saw a man who had climbed a stop sign. I think he was going to rob that building!" I thought everyone would be shocked with this information, but instead they all laughed. "See if I tell them next time!" I thought to myself.

I loved the first grade. God continued to look out for me as the sunrise of my education was peeping over the horizon and I was happy!

Chapter 10

Off to the land of milk and honey

Our home in McFarland, California

In the early forties, it seemed my dad was always looking for greener pastures. The Depression had caused things of life to sort of wither and die on the vine and the grown ups kept trying to come up with some sort of way to make a living. My dad lacked only three hours to completing his four-year-college education. He had taught for awhile, gone to seminary a year and then had to take a job in a filling station to eke out a living.

We had moved to the farm, my dad's home place, and I thought life was pretty good. My parents kept asking me if I would like a little sister since my older sister had been killed a few years before. "I guess it would be all right." I thought, but I really was okay being an only child. I got a new sister anyways.

One day I noticed a strange car drive up the rutty driveway to our farmyard. A couple I had never seen before got out of the car and walked up to the screen door of our large two-story farmhouse. I was a curious six-year-old and listened in the background.

All I could figure out from what I heard is that they were from some place called California. The way they talked about it, I thought "It must be a gorgeous place where people could have anything they wanted!"

Whatever it was my dad's cousin said, it must have intrigued him 'cause a short while later, he told me we were going to move there!

"How exciting!" I thought, and could hardly wait for moving day to come!

"First," my dad told me, "We have to have a farm auction and sell all our stuff. It costs too much to move it all that far!"

We proceeded to paint the old farm machinery while mom burned all the stuff we no longer needed. The tin cans and things that wouldn't burn were thrown under the shelter belt near our house. That was the way we took care of extra trash in those days.

The rest of our stuff, including my wicker doll buggy and Shirley Temple doll, my red tricycle, table and chairs, was polished up so it could be sold.

People came from near and far to see what we had. The auctioneer stood among the buyers and fascinated me with his funny talk. He usually told a funny story in the beginning so everyone would listen. I couldn't understand the fast talk but I noticed some of the people shook their head from time to time and crowded around to gawk at what was being sold while they sipped cokes from bottles. Occasionally, the auctioneer would holler "sold" and they went on to the next item.

The auction must have done well because before we went to our grandparents place to stay a couple of weeks, my dad had bought an almost new '39 Mercury.

When we got ready to leave for the golden state, dad packed the back seat with all our bedding, dishes, clothes. My little year -old sister and I crawled on top of all the stuff and that was our perch for all of three and a half days as we drove to California. When we finally entered the state of milk and honey, I was surprised there weren't bands out playing and people tossing their money around. It looked pretty plain, especially when we entered the desert.

We arrived at the place where his cousin Ike lived near a town called McFarland, on Highway 99. The front lawn had nice green grass. There were two big palm trees in the front yard with a nice, cloth-covered grown up swing couch. "This is really living!" I thought to myself, thoroughly impressed.

My dad was going to work for my cousin-uncle Ike. We moved into a neat bungalow house in the little town.

It had a huge yard with an almond tree, a fig tree, pomegranate bushes and a small grape arbor. I knew I would love it here.

We had a good location, on the corner was a little white church where I could attend Sunday School. Across the street was the Kern County Library where I could check out and read all the books I wanted. School was only 2 blocks away.

I did, however, wonder how long we would stay at this place. Would I ever find the answer to the meaning of life and how I could really know I could go to heaven someday? Only God knew and time would tell!

Chapter 11

A Day in infamy remains vivid

**Kern County School I attended in California
in 2nd grade**

It was December 7, 1941. I noticed how bright the California sun was as I walked along the sidewalk in front of the Kern County Library in McFarland, California. The shadows of the leaves made a diamond pattern and sparkled in the sunshine.

It was the same day the Japanese bombed Pearl Harbor. The next day, President Roosevelt gave his famous speech calling it "a date which will live in infamy!"

I was thinking about what the morning news we had heard on the radio meant!

I was only eight years old and had been attending the second grade in the Kern County Elementary School. Our family had moved from the Kansas farm to the golden state just that previous summer. I had seen a few newsreels at the movies and saw how the planes would fly overhead and drop bombs. "Will they drop bombs here?" I wondered.

As the days progressed, I could hear the little planes fly overhead more and more as the pilots from Bakersfield practiced their flying. It always gave me a strange feeling to hear the motors rev up as they made a short dive. Sometimes, when I heard the drone of the engines, I would sing "You are my Sunshine" as loud as I could so I couldn't hear them. Soon, our little town was having blackout drills, and it was spooky at night when there were no lights.

In the back of my mind, I wondered what Christmas would be like this year. I had persuaded my parents to attend the Christmas program at the little church where I attended Sunday School. I felt a sense of peace in spite of all the news of the war.

In a few months my dad decided to get a job in a defense plant in Pittsburgh, California. It was told that they could earn the mighty sum of one dollar an hour. He and my girlfriends' father drove up and would come back sometimes on weekends. My friend and I would ride our scooter to the edge of town and watch the cars come down Highway 99, looking for the right one. As we waited, we made up stories about what was happening in our universe.

I can remember walking down the sidewalk on another day and thinking about the fact that we had heard of a terrible man named Hitler. I wondered what this world was coming to, with madmen like that trying to take over the world. Would he be able to do it? I hoped not.

My mother rented out the front bedroom of our house to a young couple with a little girl. It was fun to come home after school. Mom would be sewing in the living room as would the other lady. Of course, mom always had a snack ready for me and I would eat it before I'd take my little two year old sister and the other girl out to play. Mom sewed me pretty little dresses by hand.

I loved attending the second grade. The door to our classroom opened to the outside and we had a really nice teacher. She lived only a block from us, and sometimes I would go visit her.

Our little town had a Schneider Drug Store and that was a fun place to go since one of my classmate's father owned it. There was also an outdoor fruit market where you could buy grapes for 10 cents a pound.

A hardware store stood on the corner, a place I could always go when I lost a nut off my scooter. The owner would charge me only two or three cents. One day he told me that someday it would take a dollar to buy what we could buy for a nickel then. I mulled that one over many times in my mind, but it has come to pass.

Life was interesting, even though we worried about the war. I was still learning more about God and hoping someday I would know the answers to life!

Chapter 12

I first went fishing!

A fishing trip in Colorado, after I grew up
and knew how to fish

My hubby, John, has always loved going fishing and can remember casting a line with his dad many times in his growing up years. Yes, it is a sport he has always loved.

My first fishing expedition was not with my dad in the Little Arkansas River, like John had enjoyed. I was an eight-year-old in 1942; my dad had taken a job in a defense plant in Pittsburgh, California. We had been living in McFarland but because of the war, moved to this busy place by an ocean inlet. Rentals were scarce and when my dad found us a third of a house, my mother packed my little sister and me and we moved by bus to this hectic town by the ocean.

The apartment was certainly not one you read about in storybooks, but at least our family was together. The location was just two blocks from the ocean and I was used to exploring things on my own. I would walk out to the pier and noticed that many of the people sat there with poles in the water. I'm not sure if I really knew that they were catching fish. Still, I thought I'd try my hand at it and pretend to be one of them. I usually found a bamboo pole laying around with some kind of string tied to it and a little piece of metal, so I would pick it up and throw it into the water like the others did. I doubt if I would have known what to do had a fish decided to bite the string.

Needless to say, I always went home empty handed.

It wasn't until after I'd married John that I realized what a fisherman is really like. I did go fishing, sometimes, but remember, I am one who likes to talk and do things and this is not a sport that embraces that philosophy.

Through the years, I tried my best to like fishing. One year we went to Rainbow Falls in Colorado. John helped me put a piece of cheese on the hook but that fell off. I made a casserole for the fish by wrapping the cheese around a red salmon egg and threw it in. It actually worked because it wasn't long and I felt the tug. I jerked it up and behold; I had a beautiful Rainbow Trout! This was getting to be fun!

I looked at the fish on the end of my line for awhile and watched him as his flapping around finally began to slow down. "Now what?" I wondered.

"Where had John disappeared to?" I questioned myself. "Hon," I called, "would you help me take this fish off the hook?" I'd forgotten how a voice echoes across the lake. A dozen fishermen looked up with a grin, but John was nowhere to be found. I finally had to walk about half a mile to another lake until I found the elusive John to take the fish off the hook. My conclusion: "If fishing involved taking that squirmy thing off the hook, forget it!"

Another time John and I went to Galveston, Texas, on a vacation. We had made a deal with each other. I would go deep-sea fishing if he would go to Six Flags with me.

It started out fine. John took his Dramamine the night before. We got out on the fishing boat early in the morning and headed fifty miles out. We wondered about the couches in the galley but forgot about them as we stood out on the narrow deck. I had to hold on to a thick pole with one hand and onto the rail of the fishing boat with the other. The waves got pretty high that day. The captain came by and made me catch three fish, the number they guaranteed. I caught three Red Snappers.

But something seemed a little off. About every fifteen minutes John would disappear for a little while and I couldn't figure out why. Lunchtime came and I went into the galley for some lunch. Finally it dawned on me what the couches were for! Seasick people would take turns getting their stomachs back in order! As soon as we got back to land, John's face turned pink again!

I guess weather doesn't bother John when he's fishing but motion does. Right now, I make a motion that my fishing is of the past, that is, unless John wants to go to Six Flags with me again. I may be open to bribes!

It's probably a good thing that God made each one of us different. It adds to the adventure of life, don't you think?

Chapter 13

Families struggled during WW11

Doris and Carol Kroeker

World war 11 brought a lot of changes. Life was difficult when my dad worked in the defense plant in 1942 and we lived in a third of a bungalow house in Pittsburgh, California. My folks finally decided that place wasn't safe, especially when some thugs tried to grab my mom when she went to the grocery store. She hit 'em hard, however, with her purse. My folks bought a small camper. It was in a camper park near a little town of Ambrose, about 10 miles out of Pittsburgh. I started school out there. It's the only time I remember disliking school. It really wasn't that bad, just different.

The camper was just one little room and it was crowded with the four of us. Dad went to work every day and mom kept our little home going. She baby sat a neighbor boy and so in the evening, she and I were at his house. He and I played checkers and then mom put him to bed after she made him and me drink some warm milk (I hated warm milk!)

I found a little church a few blocks away and attended Sunday School every week. The teachers were nice but I never could find the answer I was looking for.

Then my dad's cousin, Ike and his wife, Stella, visited us again. Since there wasn't room for all of us in the camper, mom put the kitchen table and chairs outside the trailer and fried bacon and eggs on the two-burner stove. Ike talked my folks into going back to McFarland.

This time, my dad was Ike's bookkeeper in his oil business and mom and I ran a little grocery-station-cabin place he owned. We lived in a large room in back of the store. I helped wait on customers and mom filled in gas.

My second cousin, Norbert, and his family lived in back of the court, and he always made a point to be around at suppertime. Mom was a good cook.

Then one day, in late fall, my dad told me that we were moving back to the Kansas farm, and I was ecstatic. I had enjoyed all the new experiences that living in California brought, but I really loved the farm. Besides, I was still looking for my answers about whether there was really a heaven and I felt like I would have a better chance in the sunflower state.

We started out for Kansas with the same tires we had driven to California two years before. The War ration board would not approve the purchase of new tires. We had to stop in Riverside, California, where dad did some patching. We drove in the mountains and it was snowing much of the time. My sister and I were again packed into the back seat with all our household belongings.

After two or three days of difficult driving, we entered the state of Oklahoma and the snow was really coming down hard. Dad had the windshield wipers going full blast so he could see the road.

Dusk had already come and gone, and the dark descended heavily on our little family, trying to make it home for Christmas.

My parents spotted a light in the distance. It was a welcome sight to see a filling station and cabin court in the snow that had almost reached blizzard proportions by now.

We were so thankful to have made it this far, and my sister and I were glad to get inside our little motel. the room was lit by a bare light bulb in the middle of the ceiling. Mom struggled into her galoshes and tramped over to the little grocery store in the station, to pick up some food for supper.

Dad fixed the patches on the tires in the filling station garage. When he came in much later, he looked tired, but he grinned at me. "Mission accomplished!" Mom had fixed our supper of hot cocoa and sandwiches and we eagerly ate them down.

The dim light of the lonely bulb gave a soft glow. Afterwards, we sang a few carols and opened our gifts. I got a gold locket and a New Testament, Just what I had wanted. My sister got a doll.

By today's standards, it could be said we were deprived. By our standards, we were safe and happy, together and we had a God who watched over us, in whatever state we were in. We were rich!

It was late afternoon on that 1943 Christmas Day when we made it into Kansas, bad tires and all. There was still a war on, we had very little money, but we were truly blest!

Chapter 14

The old farmhouse was best place to live

Grandma and Grandpa & Herb Kroeker at the farm

As the Kansas wind picks up in velocity today, it takes me back to earlier times when we lived on the farm. Although none of the buildings are there now, I can still see them as if it were yesterday.

The two-story farm house, perched on top of a Kansas hill, stood strong and stalwart, a sentinel guarding the earth space of the occupants within.

In this building my fondest memories occurred. It was here I learned how to stand against the winds of adversity, to point my face into the wind and plunge ahead. In these surroundings I learned the greatest lesson of all, how to think.

We moved into this house when I was just out of kindergarten, a city kid, with no idea how to gather eggs, feed the chickens, tend a garden or walk to school in a snowstorm. I learned fast, however, and began to love the old house in which my father grew up. Our stay at this farm was interrupted by two years of living in California, but when we came back, I loved it twice as much.

I loved the big family kitchen, the little pantry to the side, the parlor and the three or four bedrooms downstairs. We no longer used the upstairs (five more bedrooms) of this giant house, and it boasted a multitude of treasures: trunks and boxes of old clothes, books and a lot of miscellaneous stuff.

The narrow, winding steps to the second floor were the perfect place to play whenever my girlfriend came over for an afternoon or my cousin stayed for a week. We'd dress up in the old clothes we found in the trunk and pretend to be some famous person. We'd wind up an old Victrola by hand and play the one record we had found, "Blest Be the Tie that Binds."

While we played, the Kansas wind whistled forlornly through the semi-caulked windowpanes. Though an eerie sound, it also comforted us to know we were safe and snug in the house on the hill. Our imaginings gave our dreams wings to many different places. We made up plays about an old farm lady and a hobo. Both couldn't hear very well and we'd fall down laughing to the floor when we thought it really funny.

We read love letters that had been stored in the boxes and developed an insight to the characters who had written them. No one bothered us, so we had a delightful setting to test our imagination.

As my teen-age years approached, I had a yearning for my own upstairs room. My mother made one purchase: a gallon of cream colored paint. I brushed it on the wall, the old wooden floor and on an old two-seated school desk. An old iron bedstead and springs were put together and we scrounged up an old mattress. We found some old lace curtains and an extra kerosene lamp and my room was complete. The heating came from the chimney wall that came up from the first floor's coal stove. Of course, a heated brick at night kept my feet warm and toasty.

I put the desk in front of a small, square window that looked out on the farmyard. On my Big Chief tablet, my life actually took wing as I thought and wrote. I scribbled stories of adventure, of passion, at least as much as I knew in my limited world.

Outside the Kansas wind sometimes wrought havoc on the farmyard. A small tornado took the garage and set it twenty feet away from the house. The feisty wind struck part of the outside kitchen, located next to the house, but it never touched our strong structure.

I could see out on the mulberry trees that grew on one side of the long, rutty driveway that ran up the hill to our house. Occasionally someone would stop by the road to pick some of our luscious purple mulberries that had been brought here by our ancestors in 1874. Since it was also my job to pick this delicious fruit for mom's mouthwatering pies, it also added fuel to my story plots. The pickers became the sinister character in my prose. Having no television in those days, "sinister" meant anything or anyone that we didn't know personally.

It was here in this little parcel of time, cocoon-wrapped in dreams and aspirations, I learned to write about my feelings and talk to God uninhibited.

Even though time has moved swiftly on, it only takes a moment, the sound of a meadowlark, the smell of fresh rain, the wind whistling through the storm door, to take me back to one of the best places of my life, the two-story farmhouse.

Chapter 15

The fair was a magical experience

The ferris wheel

The sparkling lights of the Kansas State Fair have again mesmerized our fair city into a galaxy of sparkling rays. Waves of memory swept out from its scintillating, dazzling brightness that shone out from the turning of the Ferris wheel to the brightly-lit carousel, bobbing up and down in magical fashion. As a child in younger days, I was so intrigued with the glamour of the bright lights of the fair. It signified all the hopes and dreams for the future that I had envisioned and hoped for. As our family drove down Plum Street, I would pretend that I was going to the fair, to stay as late as I wanted, and to spend money on anything and everything. It was magic and mysterious and mythical, all rolled into one exciting experience!

I can remember going to the fair in the forties. Even though, we all worked diligently hard on the farm and dad worked at Cessna, money was not easily had during this time. Mom had to plan out how we were going to go, how to get some money and how to work out the transportation.

Mom had it figured out. We all arose even before the rooster crowed her wake up call. My parents caught three or four old hens and put them in gunnysacks and put them in the trunk of the car. Mom, my little sister, Carol, and I all rode along with dad as he drove down the driveway, Sunrise Road, around the curve by the river, past Medora, and finally to the Schultz' Produce in Hutchinson, a block off of East 4th. I guess some money changed hands for the hens and we had our spending money. Dad drove us to the Fair grounds as the sun was beginning to rise and then he made his way to work.

The big plan was we were to meet my mom's sister, Olga, and my two cousins, Dickie and Johnnie. They, too, had hitched a ride from Buhler and they would go back with us when dad picked up up after work. Since dad worked a twelve-hour shift, that would be the length of our stay at the fair.

The sun beat down unmercifully as we wended our way through the Mid-Way to the Grandstand during the day. In the afternoon, we sat down under some trees on the ground and tried to get cool. A water fountain nearby helped to assuage our thirst. Our mothers told us we could choose two rides to go on. We all voted for the merry-go-round and I think we all enjoyed that.

I had a little of my own money and told everyone, I was going on the Ferris wheel. Dickie and Johnnie were impressed when I bragged later what fun it was to look out over the whole countryside. I could see they wanted to go, too, but were too afraid. Finally, Johnnie, my younger cousin, braved the ride and he, too, thought it was wonderful. We both tried to talk Dickie into going but for some reason, he was too chicken to ride it! We finally gave up.

Our mothers had brought some food along and so at noon, we sat on the grounds of the fair and ate our fried chicken and potato salads. Mom had also brought a chocolate cake with fudge frosting and Dickie ate a lot of the frosting off. I told him he shouldn't but he did it anyway. He was funny that way. Besides, I knew my mom sure made a good fudge frosting and it did taste like candy.

As I think about it now, I am amazed we didn't get food poisoning or heat stroke or anything else along that line. We were probably toughened to the living of the forties. We didn't even think of germs or that we needed to wash our hands in the germicide of today. No one had ever told us we could get sick!

I know that God looked out for us and kept us from getting ill. He must have had a purpose for us.

When my sister Carol and I visited the fair this year, we enjoyed it very much but when it started to rain, we made a run for it! We made it to the tram that drove us around the outside of the grounds and then we ran for our car. We certainly didn't have to spend a twelve-hour day like we did in the forties. I wonder, are we getting soft in the world we live in today?

Maybe we are just "fair-weather" people!

Chapter 16

A dream realized

We all had dreams, especially in the old days. It was those dreams that gave our life substance.

The country road by our farm stretched out, strips of clay-colored burlap winding around the dark soil of the surrounding farmland.

Sometimes, when the roads hadn't been graded for awhile, the ruts in the thoroughfare could almost swallow you up, should you be unfortunate enough to get caught in its treacherous jaws.

The calendar on the wall of the big country kitchen showed 1944, and I was eleven years old. A gangly, young farm girl who was growing too fast and outgrowing her made-over clothes at breathtaking speed.

I did a lot of running, walking and skipping over the roads to get to and from school, to herd the cattle, to do my chores. I didn't mind, however, and actually enjoyed it.

I did, however, dream of someday owning a bike on which I could skim over the road, and get to where I wanted to go much faster.

One day, as my dad and I were standing by the windmill, I got up the nerve to consult with my investment planner as to how a bike could become a reality.

Dad's eyes squinted as he gave it some serious thought. He put the milk bucket down and looked out over the barnyard. The cattle were trying to outmaneuver one another and get to the hay we had just thrown down. The smell of the barnyard filled our nostrils and had become a commonplace odor. Still, I waited for his answer with baited breath.

"I'll tell you what, Doris," my dad said, "When we have our next batch of pigs, I'll let you have one to raise. After we sell it, you can use the money for a bike!"

The proposition sounded good to me and I went running to the house to tell mom. I looked forward to the birth of the piglets so I could get started.

Raising a pig was not easy, I found out. Pigs have a way of getting out of the fence and it is not easy to get the slippery creatures herded back into their pen. I spent many extra hours feeding him some extra table scraps to fatten him up. Finally, the day came when dad took him to be sold.

I could hardly wait for dad to get home with the money and when I was given a twenty dollar bill, I felt like a millionaire.

Buying a bike in the forties was not an easy task. the war had made luxuries like bicycles very scarce. I knew we had to find a way.

My father and I attended some farm auctions together. We heard that the Ratzlaffs were to have a farm sale and we determined to go. Sure enough, their son, Arnold, had his bike auctioned off. We bid up to fifteen dollars before the auctioneer hollered "Sold!"

At last, I was the proud owner of some personal transportation. I didn't care for the black color, however, so I spent the rest of the money on some maroon and white paint and a seat cover. With great care, I painted a white stripe on each side of the broad fenders after I had brushed on the maroon. Although it wasn't perfect, it was mine and it was painted in the Buhler colors.

But now I had to learn to ride the thing! I found a perfect spot to get on, by the edge of our tall front sidewalk. After wobbling a bit I could get up speed and coast down the long driveway to the road, skimming past the mulberry trees and missing the ruts, most of the time.

A few dozen skinned knees later, I had mastered the balancing act and I was ready for the road test. I knew that if I could stay balanced from our mailbox to the Goertzens down Sunrise Road, it would be easy from there, because then the road swooped down a hill to the highway.

Wobbling a little, I slowly teetered down the country road until I came to the tope of the hill. I began my descent and kept going faster and faster. The wind whistled through my ears and brushed my long hair straight back. The trees whizzed by and I felt like a bird, soaring down from the sky.

Finally I reached the highway and I came to a stop without falling. My dream of getting and riding a bike had been realized!

But then I had to walk the bike back up the hill and I knew that God had taught me another lesson from life. What goes down must come up.

Or is it the other way around!

Chapter 17

I got around

The Buhler Frolic
L to R: Ervin Unruh, Harvy Thiessen, Ruth Friesen, Doris
Kroeker, Kenny Dirks, Margie Janzen, Johnny Goertzen,
Charles Dirks, Susie Janzen, Leona Unruh, Wayne Goertzen
& teacher, Charlene Unruh

My dad, being the only driver in the family and
working two jobs, couldn't really take me anywhere,
but now that I had a bike, I didn't mind. I had another
avenue of travel! The problem, however, was that the
country school of Sunrise was somewhat on a hill, which
was pretty hard to pedal up. Sometimes I walked up the
hill, balancing my transportation, which was the last
part of my journey. When I arrived at the school, I
parked my bike next to the front porch cement slab and
left it for the day.

Those of you who have attended a country school can remember some ornery kids who have attended. Sunrise was no exception!

One day, after school, I grabbed my dinner bucket and the paper sack with my books and went to pick up my bike. To my dismay, both tires were flat. I heard one of the other girl's snicker and knew right away who was the culprit and the instigator of the foul deed. I had to walk my bike to the farm near by so I could borrow their tire pump. I felt agitated that someone could make life even tougher than it was but I knew I had to get over it.

From that day on, I didn't ride my bike every day, only when I was in a hurry. Besides, it was fun to walk with the other kids going my way.

As late September rolled around, we were busy at the school, making pictures for the Buhler Fair. I took my Big Chief Pencil Tablet and box of crayons at school and did a crayon drawing of a girl standing by a pond in the country with her dogs standing nearby. The teacher entered it as one of the exhibits at the fair.

At home I made other entries: some rice crispy squares and some delicious chocolate fudge, as well as cupcakes. Everything was made from scratch, since mixes had not yet been invented. We managed to get them to the right place in Buhler so they could be judged. I can't remember how we achieved that. Perhaps I took them to school and the teacher took them. At any rate, I was anxious to see what ribbons I had received, especially after being told they gave money prizes along with the ribbons.

The only problem was how was I to get from our farm to the little town of Buhler to receive the prizes, if any, and to receive the ribbons and the checks.

Mom couldn't drive, dad was at work and I was desperate. Did I rant and rave and kick and scream? Of course not as that would have done absolutely no good. If I wanted to go, I had to figure it out.

At last, the solution came to me, I could ride my trusty old bike! The only thing I really feared was that a dog would come running after me. For some reason, I didn't like strange dogs. I could, however, take a stick along and that would scare any potential danger from gouging into my leg. I would pedal on a wing and a prayer!

I found out what time on Saturday they would disperse the prizes in the lumberyard of the Lindas Lumber Company. I started out at least an hour and a half before the time and pedaled the two and a half miles to my hopeful fortune. I'm also sure I didn't go as fast as our son-in-law does when he rides his bike to towns hundreds of miles. My bike was used only as a means of transportation.

As I arrived in Buhler, people were crowded onto the bleachers in the lumber yard, awaiting all the announcements. Incidentally, this was located where the present Buhler Bank now stands. I made my way through the crowd and anxiously hung around. You had to go up each time your name was read to receive the ribbons and the check. My heart was pounding so hard, I thought I would faint.

Finally, they got to the art listings. I had won a first on my crayon drawing! Then my culinary skills also paid off. I pedaled home on cloud nine with a sum of seven dollars. I was rich! But more than that, I felt a sense of achievement because I had persevered in spite of many obstacles.

My second hand, trusty mode of transportation had helped me pull it off and raising a pig had helped me do it. Most of all, it was with God's help, it was *mission accomplished!*

Chapter 18

The one-room country school

Sunrise School

Sunrise School was on top of a little hill. It was painted white and had a little tower at the top with a bell. The porch in front was made of cement and it had pipes for rails around its outside. It has a place in my memory I will never forget, even if the building has long since been removed to a different location.

When it was time to begin the day, the teacher pulled the rope and the big school bell changed us to attention. We would line up outside, march in through the outside hall where the sink and pump were located, and march to our desks. We would all recite the pledge of allegiance to the flag and the teacher would offer a prayer for the day.

Since all eight grades were in one room, it was easy to listen in on the other classes. The teacher would call for "first grade reading" and the two or three students in that grade would sit in the front seats as they were taught. This went on through all eight grades.

The older students had an ink well located in the upper right hand corner of their desk so that when they practiced their penmanship, they could dip their pen in the ink well. This made a scratching noise but no one seemed to mind.

As all eight grades concentrated on their lessons for the day, two old gentlemen peered down from their lofty pictures on the wall, frowning in consternation when we made a mistake or used our time unwisely. We felt a certain kinship to both Lincoln and Washington as they observed all the goings on of our school room.

The big pot-bellied coal stove stood off in a corner of the room, a silent observer on warm days and radiant on cold days when the classes convened around her warmth. The teacher, even when she was a young, feather-like lady, had to be chief janitor as well as teacher. It was nothing for her (or him) to bundle up at recess and make several trips to the coal shed for more fuel. If the day was dark, the big kerosene hanging lamps were lit and gave a ghostly light to the room. If anyone needed to go to the outhouse, they had to weather the great outdoors to get to one of the little houses in the back.

We all looked forward to recess. When the weather permitted, we played baseball out in the pasture grass. I have a small scar on my forehead as a reminder of those bygone days. Our equipment consisted of a ball and bat and some twigs to signify the bases. One day as I played catcher, minus the mask, of course), one of the boys hit the ball with a loud thump and let the bat fly into the wild blue yonder. Of course, that's where I was standing, so I got to stop the bat from being lost in the air. A big welt soon appeared on my forehead and the next day I proudly sported a beautiful black eye.

Sometimes we had basketball fever and played vigorously out on the grass court on the north side of the school. No one actually refereed, so almost anything went. We girls were not reluctant to use our fingernails on occasion. Sometimes the recess would go a little longer because the teacher couldn't tear herself away from the game. We'd come in thoroughly steamed and sweaty and of course, some of the kids would have a few fingernail scars.

In the spring we would practice for our track meet with other country schools. The races would be run down the dusty country road in front of the school. We would also have a broad jump and high jump events. The school board would bring in some loads of sand for us in which to land. I think I was pretty good at high jump.

After recess we'd sit at our desks, cooling off, while the teacher read a continued story from books such as "Heidi." After we were cooled down, classes would again convene, starting with first grade and working on up to the eighth.

School was usually out at four o'clock and we'd trudge our way down the dusty, country road, hopefully having saved a little snack from the lunch in our dinner bucket. Sometimes some of us would stop at a little creek at the bottom of the hill and toss pebbles into the pond, voicing our dreams for the future.

Times have certainly changed since the days of the one room country school. Some for the better and some perhaps not. I will always be thankful for the privilege of attending Sunrise School and for the dedicated teachers that brought life to the term "education" in the thirties and the forties. The one-room country school will always hold a special place in my memories.

Chapter 19

Sad duties were part of farm life

Pets lived an entirely different life on our days on the farm. Living a dog's life was just that. Nothing more, nothing less. It was unheard of to take an animal to a vet in those years. We, ourselves only went to a doctor when it was a very life-threatening situation, like your finger being almost cut off, a broken leg, or perhaps pneumonia, if it was bad enough.

I can remember one fall season. Our cats around the farmyard had multiplied to practically two dozen. They did, however, roam the barn, the granary, etc. and caught the mice that tend to inhabit those places.

For some reason, the cats caught pneumonia this particular autumn and one by one, they died. We did not enjoy finding their carcasses around the farmyard. My dad, busy, of course, working two jobs, told me to bury them in back of the chicken house after school. Of course, this was not my favorite job but I seldom, if ever, disagreed as to what I was to do.

I did, however, feel they each deserved a proper burial. I would dig a hole in back of the chicken house, place the dead cat in the hole, and cover it up. It was then I would make my little three-year-old sister, Carol, and our two dogs, Shep and Spot, come and sit by the gravesite and look very sad, while I preached their funeral.

In the one room country school, I had been learning 500 Bible verses so I could attend camp in the summer. I had also been reading some monthly periodicals that came from this new evangelist, Billy Graham. I was constantly trying to find the answer concerning "Where do people really go when they die?" The answer was still not clear to me but I was learning a lot in the process. I quoted a lot of Bible verses in the course of the funeral. We also sang some hymns. After which we would adjourn to the big farm kitchen and have our funeral faspa (a German 4 o'clock lunch). Mom usually baked everyday so we always had something.

This went on for several days until all of the deceased cats had been buried. I don't remember how many cats were left but the ones who died were at least "properly attended to."

Our two farm dogs, Shep and Spot, were really not great helpers on the farm as far as herding or getting the cattle in from the wheat field or the pasture, but they were great companions to me. I think dad had picked them up as strays, thinking that we could teach them to get the cows. Somehow that never happened.

One of my jobs after school in the fall was to herd the cattle on the wheat field, making sure they did not run off to the neighbor's place. It was rather tedious to just stand around and watch them while they nibbled on the wheat. Most of the time I was by myself but on rare occasions, my neighbor, Ruth, would come over to visit. She would come out to the field with me. I had a vivid imagination so we would envision ourselves in many of life's future expectations. We could be teachers, singers, speakers, etc. and we would go through all the gyrations of our imaginary future.

As we poured ourselves into our production, Shep and Spot would jump around also, delighting in the fun of the moment.

The cattle? They barely gave us a glance and what we did was no concern of theirs as they quietly chewed their cud with a disinterested look of disdain on their faces. We didn't care, what did they know anyways!

The dogs took more part in the fun of jumping down the straw stack located by the barn. They romped and pranced around while Ruth and I threw ourselves down the soft, comfy straw. I can remember thinking this was the absolute most fun thing I had ever had!

Of course, there were times when I felt melancholy and needed someone to talk to, so Shep and Spot would always oblige. They would respond to whatever I said, be it sad or happy. They would copy my joy
or sadness, so I knew I could always count on them, except when they'd see a rabbit and have to chase it.

Thus the days on the farm were, at times, a little lonely, but not so you could notice it. It was peaceful and exciting, tranquil and scary, and I loved it. But then, I did also have God to talk to!

Chapter 20

Fears on a forties farm

**Carol, Mom and Doris
at grandma Lange's house in Buhler**

President Franklin D. Roosevelt said "The only thing we have to fear is fear itself."

His quote was cited often during the formidable 1940s, when we lived on the old farm homestead. But there were times, I felt anxiety.

There were things that frightened me...a lot. For instance, I did not like strange dogs that barked.

Whenever we would visit my grandparents in Buhler, and I wanted to walk the two blocks to my cousin's house, I just knew I would get chewed up by a dog. One of my parents or cousins would have to go with me.

I also feared a bull would chase me.

One time, on my way to school, the neighbor's cattle were out on the wheat field and the bull was pawing the ground getting ready to charge. I was mesmerized by fear, and if it hadn't been for one of the parents taking their children to school by car and stopping to ask if I wanted a ride, I just know I wouldn't be here today.

My mother wasn't afraid, at least not so I could tell. Because my dad sometimes worked at night, she was alone in the big two-story farmhouse with my little sister and me. Our house did not have a lock.

One dark autumn night, mom heard a car chug up the driveway and go behind the barn where we kept our tractor gas in a barrel. Gas was rationed at the time and was a treasured commodity. Mom lit the lantern and went out in the yard. She hollered out in her most fearsome voice, "Who's there?" She could hear the footsteps running to the Model A, which soon took off down our rutted driveway.

My mom enjoyed telling the story the next morning. It makes me laugh to think how she must have scared that gas stealer!

What bothered me the most is that I wouldn't please my dad. It's not that he was a hard taskmaster; I could feel the anxiety in him during those rough days of making ends meet. He depended on me to be his right hand person and it was important to me to do what was expected so he wouldn't have to worry.

One summer when I was 11, I drove the tractor during harvest while he operated the combine. He had told me not to put the clutch in when we went through the slew (a ditch in the bottom land).. I panicked when the tractor's front began to raise, and I did what I had been warned against and used the clutch. The combine was stuck, and my dad yelled at me to go home and get the shovel.

I ran home crying, in spite of myself.

We did get out eventually and I was so relieved. It was important to me to help all I could.

The job I dreaded the most was when mom and I had to kill a chicken for dinner. Neither of us liked this job. I held the chicken down with his head on the block, and mom swung the axe. I usually closed my eyes as she swung the weapon: I'm not sure what she did.

One time we didn't quite finish the job and the chicken ran for dear life. We couldn't catch him again that day, and I think his head grew back on!

Each day, it was my job to get the cows in from the pasture so they could be milked. As I walked out in the meadow, either skipping over the wild plants that grew in the pasture or deep in thought about some aspect of life, in the back of my consciousness was always the thought, "Look out for the snakes!"

Snakes were not just a A "pie in the sky" fear, but occasionally were there, curling and moving in a most disconcerting way. When I did see a tenacious reptile, I could have qualified for the Olympic team for the fastest speed in the shortest time.

To finish FDR's quotation, "The only thing we have to fear is fear itself-nameless, unreasoning, unjustified terror which paralyzes needed efforts to convert retreat into advance."

The fear factor of farming in the forties helped us advance into the 21st century of the world today.

With God's help, we can claim victory as long as he is in charge.

Chapter 21

Pride and new saddle shoes

Those of us who lived in the 40s had learned to appreciate anything new in the line of school clothes.

I certainly was no exception when we lived on the farm. Much of the time, my school dresses were made by hand by my mom and the material was from the sacks of chicken feed that came with printed material.

My shoes were usually brown oxfords. When it was warmer, I had white socks to wear, but they had no elastic threads around the top. They would often slip down unto the heel. This was embarrassing.

Sometimes, after school, some of us walked home behind the hedgerow that lined one side of the road that led to Sunrise School. I don't know why, but I would sometimes hit the heel of my foot with the other foot and it got all red and swollen in the back. It probably was because the back of my socks always slid down. My parents had even become concerned. I had to doctor it with Watkins salve almost every day. In spite of the hurt, I tried my best not to limp.

Then one day my cousin's wife, Lula, gave me some of her clothes. She had a navy blue skirt with two or three pleats on each side. Mom made it to fit. Somehow my parents scraped enough money together to buy me a red, sloppy Joe sweater AND a new pair of black and white saddle shoes as well as some white socks that would stay up. I was on cloud nine and proud, even though the Bible does say "Pride goeth before destruction!"

Walking to school, wearing all my treasures was not too hard. The cloud I was walking on was not as dark as the ones in the sky. It felt good to have something to be proud of, even if it was only a pair of shoes. All day long, I could run faster, make more baskets in our game at recess, and I think my brain could remember more things. There was something to be said about confidence! Why, I even felt like a teenager!

But then the sky really darkened and the rain came down in sheets. School was out at the usual time, and as I looked out at the storm, I determined "I am not going to have the rain ruin my new shoes!" It was late autumn and the temperature had turned pretty cool.

I took off my shoes and wrapped them in a paper bag and stuck them in my dinner bucket. I walked home in the mud barefooted, but I was so thankful I would still have my saddle shoes intact!

As I walked into the house, my grandmother Kroeker clicked her tongue and shook her head. I showed her my shoes in the dinner bucket and she nodded her head even more, "Such pride!" She heated some water on the kerosene stove and made me soak my feet to ward off any cold I might be getting from my escapade.

My mother made me some hot tea to drink and got out the Vicks Vapor Rub to put on my chest, and she put it in a spoon and made me take deep breaths from the vapor. My mother didn't even ask me why I had done that because she understood how important my shoes were to me. I don't remember catching cold, but I sure do remember those shoes and was thankful I had been able to save them. I no longer kicked the back of my heel and could walk and run normally once again.

My parents must have enjoyed seeing the happiness my two new items brought me because for our Christmas program, my parents purchased a store-bought, red wool dress and a pair of black suede shoes for me, and I thought I was the queen of Sunrise School!

I know I was proud again, but I think God forgave me since I was still growing up. In today's world, I'm sure I would have been labeled "poor" but not in my estimation. I had my parents who cared and a God who loved me! Besides all of that, I had black and white saddle shoes in good condition!

Chapter 22

The Kansas Gold Rush

Kansans will soon be "rushing for the gold" as the heads of wheat turn into a gleaming golden color. Combines will rumble out of storage and will deftly extract the grain from the heads. Trucks will motor down the roadways hauling the kernels to the elevators. The sunshine of promise will glow out to the world in all her glory. Our state is "the breadbasket of the world" and is the largest wheat-producing state in the nation. According to the Kansas Wheat Commission, nearly one fifth of all the wheat grown in the U.S. is grown right here in Kansas!

Many of our ancestors came to this area in the latter eighteen hundreds, bringing buckets of a hardy Red Turkey Wheat that they had painstakingly sorted through. It was not easy to till the soil with horses and plows but they did it, along with settling their homesteads. My great grandfather planted the hardy wheat between Buhler and Inman, followed by my grandfather and then my own father.

On my page of remembrance, I especially recall one harvest in 1948, as that was the last one we were able to work the harvest before we had to move off the farm and back to town. We were hoping, as did all the farmers, that this year's wheat crop would be good. We did need some of that harvest money to break us a little above even. I had been told by my teacher I needed glasses. That wasn't too hard to figure out, since I had to sit at the teacher's desk in order to see the blackboard.

We held our breath through the spring season, praying that the Kansas tornadoes and hailstorms would miss the farm on the hill. To my twelve-year-old mind, harvest was the golden epitome of all our dreams, the glowing fruition of all our labor, the pot of gold at the end of the rainbow.

The spring season made itself known in all her beautiful green covering and the wheat sparkled with an emerald enameling. Each day dad and I would walk out into the field to see how the wheat was doing.

Dad would walk a little ways, stoop down and feel the wheat heads' development as he tested the hardness of the kernel. His eyes would get a far away look and I wondered of what he was dreaming, should a good what crop present itself.

I had my own dreams and wondered "what would it be like to be rich?" To have a nice car, a refrigerator, an electric washing machine, a modern bathroom, and oh, yes, a telephone that always worked! Would I feel like a queen? If we were able to buy me the glasses I needed, would I see better but look ugly? Would I enjoy the world even more?"

It appeared to be a good year. The weather had been good, no major hailstorms, and no tornadoes had taken our garage as it usually did. This could be the one!

Dad's eyes took on a new sparkle as he eagerly greased the old John Deere tractor and got the aged combine into working condition. I followed him around like a little puppy so I could hand him the things he needed. He was happy so I was happy.

The dawn had just painted the sky a rosy glow one perfect June day when dad walked out to the field to test the wheat. "It's ready!" he announced.

The world on the Kroeker farm had been waiting for those very words. The old tractor was started by turning the flywheel and driven out to be hitched to the combine. We called our hired hand so he could come help. Mom started mixing up her dough for all the food she was going to make.

The tractor had a twelve-year-old driver...me. Dad got on the combine and managed the controls. The hired hand hauled the wheat in an old pick up and trailer.

"Everything is going well!" I thought as I bounced along on the tractor seat singing "Home on the Range."

Sweat poured down our faces as the sparkling Kansas wheat poured out of the spout of the combine into the trailer again and again. Soon we had a steady rhythm going spelling K-a-n-s-a-s G-o-l-d.

The afternoon of the second day, the sky began to darken just a bit. A cloud briefly blocked out the sun's rays and it felt good. The white clouds began to resemble steel wool as they grew darker and after awhile began to scratch at my dad's temperament as he began to realize what was happening. This was not the time for a storm!

Finally the dreaded rain came pelting down like bits of steel. The men hurriedly drove the load of wheat for the day into the garage so it wouldn't get soaked.

I felt I was watching a silent movie as I saw the driver back the trailer in the garage, and my dad stepped over to straighten the hitch. In horror, I saw my dad's face contort with pain as the load went over his foot.

There was more than an ache in dad's eyes. The hurt to his foot was more than torn ligaments. Our wait for harvest had again ended in vain. Everything had gone so well until now. Why did this have to happen?

We had been on the verge of fulfilling our dream but at the last minute, it had tottered back to the beginning again.

The sky cleared and as the sun peeped out of the clouds, a rainbow appeared, casting the wheat field with a golden glow. We felt better. After all, we did harvest some of the amber stocks of grain and we still had the rainbow of promise that God gives to those who believe.

And that, my friends, is the essence of the Kansas gold rush! It is not fool's gold if God is in control.

Doris Schroeder

Chapter 23

Fall cleaning a challenge on the farm

This is the time of year that those of us who are housewives begin to look around our homes. We realize that with the holidays that will soon be arriving, our place could use a little sprucing up. It is much easier in the era we now live, to undertake such a task. All we do is get out our vacuum cleaners, feather dusters, open our automatic washer and dryers, and we soon have the job done.

This job was not so easy when we lived on the farm in the forties. Fall cleaning was a huge undertaking and not a project to go into lightly. For instance, we had to carry out the living room rug to the clothesline, hang it up and beat the dust out of it. This was not an easy task. It took both mom and me to get the job done. It was good, also, for getting rid of any animosities or frustrations that lay hidden. By the time I was through beating the rug, I was too tired to care.

Then, of course, we had a huge family kitchen and dining room that had an old congoleum floor that was beginning to show wear at a lot of places. Once a week, we got down on the floor and scrubbed it so the pattern was beginning to disappear from view. You could see where the floorboards were located under the congoleum. Mom, handy with the paintbrush and a gallon of paint, would paint it a beige color for the winter. Of course, on that day, we had to stay off the kitchen floor.

It was also time to get the two pot bellied stoves ready for the winter. They needed to be shined up, the coal bucket washed out, so everything would be in readiness when the frostiness of late fall and winter would come blowing down the chimney. The stovepipes to the chimney had to be checked for clogs. If we built a fire and the pipe was stuffed, it could smoke up the house. We also had to order a load of coal to be put by the outside kitchen, so we could get to it when the time came.

The kitchen curtains in the farmhouse kitchen had to be taken down, as well as the lace curtains in the living room. We heated water on our kerosene stove, brought in our hand propelled washing machine, and washed them, starched them with a concoction we had mixed on the stove (careful it didn't get lumpy), and hung them out to dry. During this time, we washed the windows with hot, soapy water and shined them up with some old newspaper.

When the curtains were dry, they had to be pressed with the iron we had heated on the stove. It was difficult to get the iron just right, not too hot, or we could burn a hole in the curtains very easily. We carefully hung them back up without wrinkling them and we had accomplished our fall cleaning until next Spring.

Our daily chores continued every day and those were things that could not be put off. We filled the lamps with kerosene, as well as the jug by the stove for cooking. Cleaning the chimneys on the lamps was a must, so they would give enough light to read by in the evening.

When we did our morning or evening chores, we always had to be sure to bring in more coal for the heating of the stove as well pump a bucket of water at the outside pump for drinking and washing.

Another everyday chore in the morning was washing the cream separator after we had milked the cows. The milk would be put in quart jars and set in some cold water that we had also pumped outside. Since we had no electricity and in winter, no ice, this worked out quite well.

For our meat, mom always had some that she had canned, and stored in the cellar. We also had some home-canned vegetables on the shelves as well as some potatoes we had raised. We made our own butter in a large crock with a wooden pole that we beat up and own until the cream magically turned into the golden concoction of butter.

We never heard the word "bored." I doubt if we would have known what it meant, there was always so much to do. I know we did have a little extra time to read in the evening or just sit around the table and talk. I would ask my parents a lot of questions, about God, their youth and life in general.

It was, however, a great relief when we had finished the fall cleaning on the farm!

Chapter 24

Getting the news out

Little did we dream back in the forties how we would some day be able to hear the world news with a touch of the computer or television button, or the musical ring of a cell phone. Text messaging had not even been envisioned in the dream world of the smartest kid. Indeed, news of what was happening in WW2 could only be seen on movie screens and certainly didn't take us to the front lines the way our last war with Iraq began.

Our days on the farm were without electricity because the REA had not put up the electrical lines across the golden Kansas wheat fields. Our biggest news source was the big on-the-wall telephone, the battery operated radio, the occasional newspaper and by word of mouth to those who couldn't afford it.

It was no wonder that when the phone rang, it sent little chills up and down our spines. We only received calls when there was special news to be told. Most of us were on a party line, where several people were on one line. We each had a special ring...two longs and a short, two shorts and a long, etc. It wasn't surprising that when the phone rang at any time and we picked up the receiver, we could hear little clicks reverberating in our ear as everyone tuned in to the latest information. This was probably the best source of local news we had and it really wasn't considered rude to listen in, although it was irritating.

When we wanted to call out, we picked up the ear piece, turned the crank on the side and the operator would ask "Number, please!" We stood on tiptoe to answer in the mouth piece. We seldom called long distance, only in emergencies.

I remember one night, however. Mom was home alone with my little sister, Carol and I, in the old two story farmhouse with no locks on the doors. Dad was at work at the Sam Schneider filling station in Hutch and was late getting home.

Suddenly the phone sounded its grim peal in the late night. Mom had to make her way in the dark to the kitchen area where our one phone was located. I had heard it, too, and crept into the kitchen to hear what was going on. "Hello!" she shouted into the mouthpiece. It was quiet for a minute and then her eyes got big. Later, she turned to me and told me the news "The filling station burned down!"

This was scary news, because jobs were ultra scarce in those days. Dad, however, was all right and would be home shortly.

Another news item came when on April 12 of 1945, dad got home with the news that our president, Franklin Delano Roosevelt, had died. I knew our neighbors, the Friesens, didn't have a phone, so I ran the half mile to their house with this earth-shaking news. I cried along with them although I didn't really understand it all.

Sometimes the phone came in handy. Much as I hate to admit it, there was a time I didn't do my job right. Mom was to let the cattle out on the wheat field at a certain time and I was supposed to herd them in after I got home from school. One day, I purposely forgot because "I didn't feel like it!" When dad got home, later that evening, and asked if the cattle were in, I had to admit they weren't. The next day, he had to stay home from work and call around. By the time I got home from school, he had finally found them a couple miles away and I was relieved. To state it simply "It didn't happen again!"

Then, of course, there was the weather. Our battery radio was dead most of the time, so we just depended on our instincts on the weather. We had to go by the old tales of our forefathers:

If the wind changed to the north, it could snow.

If you see a tunnel coming down from some dark clouds, you better run for the cellar.

If the sunset is clear, it will be a nice day tomorrow.

If it's raining, you better run for cover or you might get wet!

It is no wonder, however, that although life was hard, we felt more at peace. We had to take life as it came. We didn't hear all the possibilities of terrorist attacks, earth warming, the economy and crime rates or even presidential elections. We just lived our life one day at a time and left it to God to help us do the right thing.

And that, my friends, is how we got the news out in the good ole days!

Chapter 25

To Grandfather's house we went for Thanksgiving

"Little" Grandma Lange

Over the river and through the wood, to grandfather's house we go, the horse knows the way to carry the sleigh, through the white and drifted snow. This legendary poem written by Lydia Marie Child near the mid 1800s, also depicted what we did on Thanksgiving in the 1930s and 40s. Only our sleigh was the car and the woods were located in the little town of Buhler.

Many times in those days, we visited both grandparents on Thanksgiving and Christmas, as they both lived in this little town. Both of our grandparents from my dad and mom's sides expected all their children to come and that we did. It was a very full day to me as I visited my cousins on both sides.

The back door slammed behind us as we entered the Lange house, located on the Main Street of Buhler. My Aunt Olga would be in the kitchen helping my little grandma get the food ready. Mom put on her apron and they continued the preparations. My Aunt Anna would be sitting on a chair and watching as they scurried around, checking the turkey, mashing the potatoes, making the gravy, and all the last minute things that went with a feast in those days.

My "Little" grandma, as I called her for the simple reason she was very petite, had spent days getting ready. Pie crust was made by hand as there were no special mixes. It took flour, lard, salt and water, and a rolling pin to get the crust just right. The cranberries had to be cooked, as were the potatoes and mashed with a hand held potato masher, until the creamy substance was just right. The whipping cream was beaten with an egg beater and took a little time to get teased into the luscious concoction that adorned the pumpkin pie.

My grandfather never talked to us grandchildren because he could only speak German and we couldn't.
I think we baffled him because he would always look at us with narrowed eyes, and I was a bit frightened. I realized later it was because of his eyesight.

Finally, the meal was ready. The grown ups all sat down at the dining room table. There must have been about 12-14 adults. We children had to wait until they were through and then we ate. I think we probably numbered about ten.

Uncle Pete, the preacher in the family would say in his deep voice "Let us pray!" Then he would pray, usually in German because that is all my grandparents could understand. Then he'd look up with a glint in his eye and say "Please pass the mashed potatoes!" We all knew what his favorite food was!

We kids watched as they filled their plates with turkey and dressing, potatoes and gravy, green beans and rolls. Each place had an exquisite champagne glass filled with strawberry Jell-o and bananas and a sparkling mound of whipped cream on top. Finally, as they got ready for their pumpkin pie with more whipped cream, they would start feeding us kids in the kitchen. What a feast!

Later, when my parents called, we got in the car and drove to the other end of Buhler where my other grandparents lived. This one I called "Big Grandma!" It really wasn't that she was large but she was bigger than my other one. My grandfather always had a little mischievous look in his eye. My memories, however, are mostly after he suffered from dementia, so I didn't get to know him well.

Their house was smaller and so we kids usually stayed down the basement. We played games and talked around the table with some of the "faspa" food on it. This was a German 4 o'clock lunch, so at that time we had some zwiebach and cheese and perhaps sugar cookies or cake. The thing we enjoyed the most was Grandma's sugar bowl. It had sugar cubes in it that we loved to nibble on.

In those days, I didn't really voice what all I was thankful for but I knew in my heart, I was grateful for all my cousins, even if we argued sometimes. I felt good that I had parents and grandparents whom I knew, cared for me, even if they didn't say it. I knew I still wanted to find out for sure how I could know I was going to heaven some day, but I somehow knew, I would find the answer.

We went home from our Thanksgiving celebration, contented and VERY full.

In spite of everything that is happening in this world 65 years later, I am so thankful my grandparents had the courage to come and settle in the United States of America!

Chapter 26

The night of the Christmas Program

The week before the Christmas program, the country school of Sunrise, began to take on a certain glow. Floor sweep was put on the floors and at recess we students would skate across the wooden boards. This would make the floor shiny for our big event.

The teacher of all eight grades would assign the artistic ones to draw Christmas pictures on the blackboards with colored chalk. This, of course, after the boards had all been washed down with hot, soapy water.

The day before, the school board chairman would arrive with a huge, pine tree and set it up in the front of the school. The pine odor permeated the air with a pungent smell that seemed to add sparkle to each of our beings. Later, the board would do the decorating so it would be a gala evening

Finally, the day of the program arrived. In the morning, mom wrapped my hair around rolled up newspaper and tied it with strips of cloth. This was the one time I wore my hair wrapped up in a scarf to school. We practiced our program and at noon, cut across the pasture and home to "rest up" before the big event of the season. It was worth the effort to have "Shirley Temple" curls for the evening.

The afternoon moved slowly by but finally it was time to get ready. I did my chores as early as I could, so I would have plenty of time to get dressed. Finally, I'd have bugged everyone enough and we got into our '39 Mercury to drive down the country road to the school on the hill.

Entering the school through the outside hall, where the pump was located, I always caught my breath. The ceiling lamps were lit and cast a golden glow in the room. Although the tree had no lights, it sparkled with the shiny Christmas balls and the heady smell of pine greeted our nostrils.

I made my way to one of the front desks that had been assigned to me, and waited for the program to begin. The roll-up curtain in front had been pulled down and we could read all the advertisements that were splashed on the side of the scenic view that had been painted on. My girlfriend, Ruth, and I busily exchanged confidences as we checked out the incoming crowd. The closer the clock came to the starting time, the more the butterflies in our stomachs began to flit around.

Eventually, the teacher caught our eye and we slipped behind the curtain with the other students. We quickly lined up the way we had practiced and as the curtain was rolled up, we sang our opening song "Joy to the World!" rang out through the walls of the little country school as we poured our hearts into our singing.

The teacher announced the numbers, some pieces by the little ones, a skit and of course, there was usually a play with a theme about "The Light in the Window!"

We usually gathered together one more time as a whole student body of twelve to fifteen students and sang the closing songs.

"This concludes our program!" the teacher announced at the end. This was followed by thunderous applause by the parents. Each one was thinking, "My child did so well!" Our parents were proud of us but they didn't voice this observation to anyone else. "It might give them the big head!" they thought.

After the program was over, we students waited breathlessly while the school board got up and went into the boy's hall. They came out with a large box of candy-filled sacks and handed one to each of us. Then they gave some to the little children and finally to the parents if there were some left over.

Ruth and I gingerly opened our twisted bags to see what was in it. We were told not to eat any so a peek had to suffice. There were two or three peanut clusters, a couple orange slices, chocolate drops, hard candy, peanuts, a few walnuts and Brazil nuts, and an orange and an apple.

Finally our parents started saying it was time to leave. The school board got ready to blow out the ceiling lamps. The magical evening of the year had come to an end. It would have to suffice to talk about the things that happened and dream about the things that didn't.

The misty glow of the evening lent itself to my imaginative mind wanderings that would again make its way into my Big Chief Pencil Tablet. I could crawl into my cold, iron bed with a heated flat iron for warmth with a real smile on my face, remembering the Christmas Program!

Chapter 27

The Christmas Sack

"Big" Grandma Kroeker

The windshield wipers of the '39 Mercury kept time with the beating of my heart as our family of four turned in the driveway of my Grandmother Kroeker's house in Buhler. It was late afternoon of Christmas Day. It had been a hard trip for us to move back from California to Kansas in the middle of a snowstorm. It had been exciting to think my favorite cousin, Della, would still be at Grandma's house, as would everyone else, for the annual Christmas celebration.

The cars were all gone, however, and my heart dropped. Always one to look forward to Christmas, this one had gone astray all the way. I began to feel as bleak as the sky that was spitting out snow pellets.

The trip to Kansas had been hard. To begin with, the rationing board in California wouldn't give us permission to replace the smooth tires on our car and dad had to do some patching along the way. We had spent Christmas Eve in a little motel in Oklahoma, Dad used the evening fixing yet another tire in the garage of the motel owner. Mom had done her part, making sandwiches and hot cocoa on a little burner in our room. It had been exciting to open our gifts; I got what I wanted, a little New Testament and a gold locket that opened up. And I felt optimistic...then.

We had left early on that Christmas morning, even plowing through some snow drifts part of the way. Carol, my little sister, and I sat on top of the bedding in the back seat of the car, peering through the lacy patterns the snow made on the windows. It had been exciting to see the word KANSAS on the sign as we entered back into the state we had left a year and a half before.

Oh sure, I had enjoyed the four different places we had lived in the golden state but in my nine-year-old mind, my heart still belonged to Kansas. The country school with all eight grades in one room were really my family and I had missed them. Then also, my cousin, Della, my playmate through my younger years, especially after my sister, Luella, had been killed, would be at grandma's and I could hardly wait.

And now, she wasn't there.

"Let's get in the house, Doris!" my dad advised. Slowly I crawled out over the bedding in the car and stepped into the cold, white, snow. Grandma, who never smiled, met us at the door and we tramped into her little kitchen.

After we were settled in, she handed me a little gift-wrapped package that "one of my cousins had left for me."

"Oh, how nice!" I thought happily as I tore the paper off the box. "Della remembered me and missed me as much as I missed her!"

The paper came off, one layer at a time and the same was true when I opened the box. Finally I got to the meat of the gift...a nickel. "It was a joke!" I reasoned, but somehow I was in no mood for hilarity. "Besides, I don't know that it came from my favorite cousin! It could have been her brother, Lou, playing a joke!"

Grandma watched my expression and went off to get something from the closet. It was a brown sack and she handed it to me, her mouth even curving up a little on the end.

Untwisting the end, I looked inside and there, nestled among all the peanuts and walnuts were some orange slices, peanut clusters, chocolate drops and pieces of hard candy. Lots of sweets for a lonely little girl who was feeling somewhat depressed.

"Thank you, grandma!" I said as I looked at her face. Her eyes had softened and the ends of her mouth curved up. She knew how to make one little girl happy with the Christmas sack.

The Christmas sack became a Christmas tradition in the years to come from both grandparents. We even received one such treat both at the school and the church programs. It was one of the highlights of the Christmas season. Its contents were rationed out for the long winter months that always followed, usually lasting until the first of March.

We didn't get sweets very often so we savored each bite of the fulfilling contents. It wasn't just the sweet candy that went into them that made them so important. It was the love that came along with the Christmas sack. God knows how to make us feel loved.

Chapter 28

A cold day in winter!

Living on the farm in the forties was definitely not an easy task. Neither was getting to school across the snow-laden wheat field painless and it sometimes took absolutely all the energy I could muster to get to school on a cold, snowy day. I did not have the luxury of a school bus or a parent to drive me the mile and a half to the country school in a warm car. My transportation consisted of my own two legs covered with cotton stockings and overshoes to get me through the snow, ice, mud and slush to the school named Sunrise on the hill. I do not remember ever turning back with the excuse "I can't make it!" If I was alive, I made it, and that was that!

One day was, however, especially bad. When I left the farmhouse at home, the wind was blowing across the yard. When I looked how far it would be to go the road route, I decided, instead, to trudge across the snow packed wheat field. Gusts of wind made the going pretty tough so I decided to angle my trail to the school road so it wouldn't be quite so far. To do this, I had to go through the slew in the lower part of the field. There were tall, snow-laden, thistle weeds I had to plough through and I wished I had gone the long way. I had a scarf tied around my face but it had turned to ice with the cold Kansas wind blowing with each breath I took.

I had noticed a little hole on the middle finger of my right glove when I left home but had not taken the time to sew it up. Now I wished I had. Since I carried my dinner bucket with that hand, it got a lot of the blustery cold North wind that sent curling snakes of snow around me with each step I took. I thought my hands were frozen into a U-shaped mass.

When I finally reached the other side of the ditches, I was beginning to wonder if I would even make it. It took every bit of resolve to continue on up the hill to Sunrise School. As I staggered up the steps to the white building, I could barely get the front door open and somehow stumble into the outside hall. It seemed most of the students were standing around and looked at me as I came in. One of the older girls took hold of my hand holding the dinner bucket and that is when everything turned black.

It seems that I had gotten frost bite on the middle finger of my right hand, where I had the hole in the glove. That was a good lesson about procrastination. The older kids got me revived, however, and we all spent the rest of the day, holding classes around the big pot bellied stove. I cannot remember how I got home after school, but I do know I had the scar from the frost bite for many years after.

Not all the snow days were as bad and we, being pretty seasoned farm kids at the time, would go outside at recess and play games like Fox and Geese in the snow. Someone showed us a new thing we could do. I had never heard of it before; we could lie down in the snow and wave our hands and feet back and forth. When we got up, we would have left an angel imprint in the soft billowy white stuff. This intrigued me and I thought this was a very smart game to play, as I could always use more guardian angels around to watch over me.

On the very cold days, we stayed in at recess and played mind games. One of them was "Grandma doesn't like Tea, so what does she like?" We guessed all kinds of things until we finally caught on...it was anything with the letter "t." We also played fruit basket upset. We were each given the name of a fruit and the one that was it would say something like "apples and oranges." The ones named that would try to exchange seats before "it" would grab it. When she said "fruit basket upset!" we all exchanged seats. Games were simple and fun.

At any rate, we enjoyed the snowy cold days of winter in the forties just as much as any other season. We knew

God was watching out for us in any kind of weather and we knew we could count on him to get us through, just as he does now.

Chapter 29

The 'friendly fire' of the potbellied stove

The Pot-bellied stove

The wind howled like a wounded coyote through the windowpanes of our Kansas farmhouse on cold winter mornings in the '40s. The crows in the shelterbelt bombarded me with their morning symphony, a sound both arrogant and melancholy. The noise of their crowing awakened my senses for the day. Would I accomplish something worth while so that later I could boast, or would their plaintive rhythm echo the loneliness that living on the farm sometimes brought into my consciousness?

The potbellied apparatus was usually burning brightly due to the efforts of my mom. She got up in the dark to feed the stove some of the coal that had been brought in the previous night.

The stove was the center of life for us when the blustery cold winter winds would blow across the wheat fields of Kansas.

Inside, the stove was the bright spot of the house and, because of its importance, had to be fed all day. If mom was pressing the starched clothes with the flat iron that had to be heated on the stovetop or I was doing my homework on the large dining table, we were always near its warmth. My little sister played with her paper dolls, cut from catalogues, nearby, and dad even did his books near the stove's inviting warmth.

Of course, there were times when I could let my thoughts wander as I watched the dancing shadows made on the wall from the flickering fire in the stove. My imagination sparkled with the contents of my writer's brain. I envisioned lively stories as the shades of gloom hop scotched across the wallpaper. Sinister characters would skim across the wall and sometimes end up in one of the stories in my Big Chief pencil tablet.

It was fun to sit around the stove after one of our few community events. Our family did not have much of a social life, but we did enjoy going to the PTA meetings at the country school. Later, the grown ups would have pie and coffee while we students would go outside and talk. When we came home from the monthly gathering, we'd warm ourselves by the stove and talk about all we had heard, just the facts, you know, not the gossip. Of course, a cup of hot chocolate added to the festivities.

As I felt the warmth of the friendly old stove spread its cheerfulness, I wondered if it ever remembered the things that were spoken around it comforting circle. It certainly was a part of the family, both at home and in school. The family circle around the friendly fire of the potbellied stove was seldom broken.

In the distance we would hear the distant call of the coyote, the plaintive wail of the train. The wind would whistle forlornly through the not-quite caulked windowpanes of the five upstairs bedrooms. An occasional squeal from the pigpen could be heard through the frosty night air.

Certainly, as in the morning light we felt a little loneliness on occasion, we had our dreams for the future. No matter what discouragements might come our way, we knew we had hope. We had a family who believed in us. Most of all, we had the joy of knowing, because we belonged to God, we had been created for a purpose. His love, like the stove, warmed our hearts and made life worthwhile.

Though we didn't have much in material goods, there were few people who did. We were content to be alive and dream about what life might be like someday as we were warmed by the friendly fire of the potbellied stove, which had become a stable part of our life.

Doris Schroeder

Chapter 30

The Treasures of the Old Barn

The Barn

To most people, it was just a big old barn. It had little windows on the side that you could see when you drove onto the farmyard. I guess they had been put there from the days when my grandfather had horses. These animals could look out and see the world as they were kept in their stalls. In fact, there was usually some left-over horse liniment on the shelf when you came in, and of course, a bridle and harness or two.

When we lived on the farm, each window had a stall and when we'd do "chores" and milked the cows, they let in a patch of light which helped us see what we were doing. It is here I was beginning to learn some of the basic things of farming. As my dad patiently tried to teach me the rudiments of milking, I tried my best to get the stream of milk going. The fact that my fingernails were a little long was not good for this particular job. Of course it would have been easier if I had cut my nails a little shorter.

My dad was much better at milking than I was and my mom was good at filling in when it proved necessary. She, of course, would always leave a little bowl of milk for the barnyard cats when she was done.

The other side of the barn was a big open space where the cattle could congregate on cold or rainy days. They would stand around in the dark shadows, chewing their cud and staring at each other with their huge, soulful eyes. The worst task in the world, I thought, would be to clean out that part of the barn with a shovel. It suited me just fine that dad never asked me to do that. Instead, that job went to the hired hand when we had one. And the smell!!! I can't believe I once thought I loved the stench of that part of the barn.

My favorite place was in the center of the barn. It had a loft by one side and usually there was some hay in it. This, of course, made ideal hiding places when my friends or cousins came over. We made up all sorts of games to play within the confines of the barn. We played hide and seek, told ghost stories, we made a stage on top in the loft and gave speeches and sang silly songs we made up. We jumped from the top into the hay down below. There was no limit to our imagination and thankfully, no broken bones from our landings.

There was one thing we did, however, that really wasn't the best. My older cousins thought it quite a challenge to hunt for hidden eggs that the chickens had somehow snuck in. To them, it was great fun to open the barnyard loft door, and throw the rotten eggs down into the yard below, smashing them in all their yucky glory.

The barn had no electricity so when my dad did the chores in the evening after coming home from work, it was my job to hold the lantern. This is the time I would pour out all my dreams and aspirations for the future. I would sing, act, talk and preach to my heart's content.

My audience? The cattle merely looked at me with their mournful expression, slowly chewing their cud and wondering "And what kind of animal is this thing!"

I didn't care. The warmth of the barn gave me comfort, my dad gave me little bits of encouragement and the cattle gave me the audience. As I opened the two piece walk-through door and looked outside at the twinkling stars, I could feel God looking down at me, and smiling.

The barn on the farm yielded lots of treasures!

Doris Schroeder

Chapter 31

One of life's solutions

Doris and friend Ruth

Have you ever thought how hard it would be in life if you couldn't drive a car? This is something we take for granted in today's world. If we are missing an ingredient in the kitchen or we need something for the house, we merely grab our purse, jump in the car, press a button for the garage door to open, and race over to the nearest store. In spite of the high price of gasoline, most of us still do it on occasion. Yet in the 30s and 40s, many women did not even know how to drive. Besides, most households only owned one car, if even that.

My mother was one of them, even though she had done a little driving in their just-married days. She had often told me the story how she had turned too short at a corner when dad was trying to teach her to drive, and had tipped over the Model T. She had never driven since that time. Knowing my mom, I know that once she made up her mind, you could not change it.

Of course, this made it pretty hard for my dad when we lived on the farm. He was the only driver and had to drive clear to work in Hutch, leaving us on the farm with no transportation.

In fact, one wintry day, when I came home from school, mom was a little agitated. Dad had been home that day, working on getting the motor of the car to spin, when it started and almost sliced one of his fingers off. As mom related it, dad came running into the house, shouting "I lost a finger, I lost a finger!" He rummaged in the buffet drawer and then took off with the car. There was a lot of snow on the long driveway but it wasn't too deep on the field to the side, having been kept shallow by the row of mulberry trees. Somehow, he had made it to the road and down to the highway, mom recounted.

She kept saying to me "I don't know if he said I lost a finger or I lost a figure and had to get to the Buhler Bank!"

Of course, our wall phone was not working at the time so we could do nothing but wait anxiously for dad's return and wonder about all the possibilities.

The sun was just beginning to set in the west in ominous-covered clouds when we spotted the familiar '39 Mercury slowly driving up the hill on the snow packed ground.

I ran out to meet dad as he got out. He grinned sheepishly but his face looked pale. He was holding his hand gingerly and I noticed a thick bandage on the middle finger of his right hand. We came into the house and he told us what had happened. "The top part of my finger was almost cut off when the motor started up. I knew I had to get to the doctor in Buhler before I passed out. I prayed I wouldn't get stuck as I took off down the field and I managed to get there all right, but just barely!"

If I remember correctly, mom had to milk the cows that night and probably the rest of the week, and of course, I helped.

As I look back now, I marvel at the persistence my dad had to have to keep going at a time when it seemed there was not much hope. There were so many obstacles he had to overcome. He had studied to be a teacher and was only 3 hours short of a college degree. He had wanted to enter seminary to become a preacher and they told him he was too old at thirty, now he worked in a filling station and farmed. He and mom had lost a daughter a few years earlier by an accidental shooting, now he just had me and Carol, another girl. He could have used a boy to help him on the farm, but he had me instead. Last of all, he was the only one who could drive in a time when he needed help, badly.

Recalling those days, I can understand now what trying times he must have had. A person tends to forget the rare times that he yelled at me, because he must have had burdens pretty hard to bear. He did depend, however, on a God who could see him through times that were certainly not easy and I'm sure it was God who gave him a solution to all of his problems. One of them was to teach me, a young ten-year-old girl to drive, but then, that is next chapter's memory, so look out!

Chapter 32

Look out for an eleven-year-old driver!

My dad needed another driver badly when we lived on the farm in the forties. Since I was the only one around who could even slightly meet that criteria, I was elected to do it. Learning to drive was a little different than in today's society. Now, you take a driver's ed. class in high school and when you are 16, you go in and take a test. My experience was a little different.

Driving instruction began on the farm yard. Dad told me to push my foot on the one pedal, pull the gear shift down and then to the left, let up on the clutch slowly and hopefully, the car would be rolling. All right, that accomplished, I had to recall where the brake was. Sometimes I didn't remember until we had already hit the old hayrack, the stock tank or something else on the farmyard. Every time I started to move, the chickens ran out of the way, like roosters with their heads cut off, squawking all the way. Our two dogs, Shep and Spot, sat off at a distance since they didn't want to get hit. I must admit our '39 Mercury was quite accommodating to the whims of an eleven-year-old.

I don't know why but after awhile my dad seemed to think I should practice out on the wheat field. We opened the gate from the barn and drove out where we had more room for mistakes.

Again our car went through many grinds and grumbles as I learned the rudiments of changing gears and backing up. You understand that automatic shifts had not yet been invented, and it took a lot more knowledge to drive a car in those days.

Finally, my dad let me drive down the country road which took a lot of expertise, because I had to dodge the big ruts in our driveway. A couple times, I didn't miss them and dad had to get the car relocated.

He began to let me drive when we went to visit our relatives on Saturday or Sunday afternoon. I always felt so elated when he would ask "Do you want to drive, Doris?" I felt it was an honor and even though I always felt some trepidation, I was thrilled when I had the opportunity.

One Sunday afternoon, we were driving to nearby Newton to see my aunt and uncle, Mary and George Schierling. We were traveling down Highway 50, mom and my little sister, Carol, were in the back seat and dad was snoozing in the front. I was zooming along fine at 50 miles an hour.

I really felt grown up and probably a little proud that I could drive so well. Suddenly, the turn off to Halstead came up. I couldn't remember whether this was the right corner, so I began the sharp turn while calling out to my dad "Is this where we turn or not?"

The car careened wildly on two wheels and almost turned over. Of course, dad woke up suddenly and grabbed the wheel and mom and Carol screamed passionately in the back.

Our trusty old car managed to right itself as I remembered how to stop. My mom was still screaming, dad looked pale and my little sister was crying. My hands were shaking as we took stock of the situation and I secretly vowed I would never drive again.

In spite of mom's protests, dad told me I could continue driving. My hands were still shaking as I backed up and continued down highway 50. I can remember looking at the graveyard as we drove by and thinking "Dad is so wise by making me drive because if I didn't, I might never want to again!"

Actually, I was more cautious after that. I think it was when I was 13, we drove up to what was later the Self Service Drugs and is now a train store, and I went in, filled out a brief form and for the grand sum of one dollar, was issued my first driver's license. To me, that was an accomplishment. My dad? He deserved a medal of honor, but then, of course, he now had another driver in the family.

I am sure, however, that before each trip we took, dad was quietly praying for God to keep us safe. And he did! I'm still here, however, the '39 Mercury is long gone to who knows where!

Chapter 33

From a wedding to a funeral

Life must be understood backward, but it must be lived forward! - Kierkegoard. This piece was written in later life – just last year as a matter of fact...

The last two weeks have been a time of deep reflections, even during all the phases of happy, sad, nostalgic and memorable times. We have experienced the happiness and joy of two young people starting out on their road of life, felt the pangs of childhood slipping from their shoulders and embarking on the future, full of hopes and dreams.

Flying to Florida, we experienced the happy and sad emotions that go with a grandson's wedding. Arriving back at the Wichita Airport, we received the news that a dear sister had passed away and we would be attending her funeral in a couple days. We felt the bitter sweetness of having identified with her and yet knowing we will never see her in this life time again. We take pleasure in the memories of living we enjoyed with Helen but now that is all we have left.

These were two extreme scenarios of life within a short length of time. Each needing to be dealt with in a different way.

Our second youngest grandson, Jason, and his bride, Becky, walked around all the pre wedding festivities with a big smile on their faces, fully confidant that life is wonderful. They had, with the help of their diligent parents, got all the thousand and one wedding details down pat and ready. I was again amazed at the details a wedding in this day and age demands. Everything went well, just as the wedding of another grandson Ryan and Melissa's wedding had been in March.

It was when I saw three of our grandsons as well as our son on the wedding platform of their church in the black tuxes and red ties that I felt a pang of bitter sweetness. The grandsons are now "center stage" as they begin their life's journey. Our son and his wife are now the ones guiding them and John and I are the ones sitting back on the side. "Have we done our job right? Can they now face the world and be the people God wants them to be?" Only time will tell.

The little three- year- old flower girl performed her job beautifully. The only problem being her dress was too long and they showed her how to hold it up a little as she walked. The trouble was, she only had two hands. Walking down the aisle holding her dress in one hand

and the basket of rose petals in the other, she had no more hands to drop the petals on the floor. This bothered her, so she dropped a whole bunch of petals right by the stage. She was starting out in life doing the best she could.

During the ceremony the bride sat at the piano to sing a song she had written to Jason. He, in turn, read a poem to her that he had written. I noticed they couldn't really look at each other too much during their renditions because their hearts were too full of love and they thought they would lose their place.

After the reception at the cultural center, we all saw them off in a maze of soap bubbles that glistened and shone in the hot Florida sun. One wonders what their life will be like and will they be able to do the things God has planned for them.

With our contemplative thoughts, we flew home on Tuesday. We had not even had too many delays on the plane and got to the Wichita terminal to pick up our luggage. We spied our niece, Jolene, who was the flower girl at our wedding fifty six years ago. She and her husband Rich were also waiting for some luggage of one of their daughters. She took one look at us and with a hug, told us "You don't know, do you?"

Then she told us that her mother, Helen Loepp, our sister, had passed away while we were gone and her funeral would be in two days.

My mind could not at first comprehend this news. Helen and I had been to the beauty shop together the day before we left. She had a busy week planned and it seemed incomprehensible. She was always so busy and ready to go places. All the sisters had been at her house the week before celebrating a birthday. It couldn't be!

But it was and we did attend her funeral on Thursday. The last two weeks we saw the beginning of a couple's life together and the end of someone's life...all people we loved. Is it sad? You better believe it. The good thing is we all do know the God who created us and we know that was his plan and we do not question it.

Looking back, we halfway understand. Looking forward, we trust God.

Chapter 34

Life's Biggest Decision

Doris finds the answers

To say we moved around a lot in my younger years, is an understatement because by the time we were getting ready to move back to Hutchinson, I had thoroughly loved living on the farm two different times. Since the farm was my dad's home place, it, too, was my favorite place in the 12 places we had lived in my childhood.

If you recall in the second chapter, when my sister was killed in 1936 and I was told Luella had gone to heaven, I had a lot of questions about that place. I don't think, however, that my parents knew just how to answer that, although, they did try to help me find the answer. It seems to me now that at that time, accepting Christ and going to heaven was a deep secret that you had to discover for yourself. I had certainly done my share of looking for the answer. When we moved to California and different places in the golden state, I had always found a church with a Sunday school I could attend, hoping for the solution. The SS teachers were always very loving and nice, but no one really gave me the answer with any certainty. In retrospect, it probably was because I wasn't really ready.

Back on the farm, I sometimes attended revival meetings with our neighbors, the Friesens. The evangelists of that day talked about where I'd go if I didn't choose heaven. Hell sounded awful and I knew I didn't want to go there. Somehow, it just didn't come clear to me and I was worried. At some special service, I even went forward, thinking that must be the answer. Still, nothing happened. Someone asked me if I had prayed through, and I finally said I had but I knew it wasn't true. I didn't really know what "praying through" meant.

The teacher we had at Sunrise that year was a Christian lady by the name of Esther Willems. She got us involved with the Rural Bible Crusade and I learned 500 Bible verses so I could go to Bible camp in summer. As I learned the verses, the truth of the Bible was finally becoming more clear to me.

Then, one beautiful, crisp Autumn day, as I walked home from school across the wheat field, the thought of heaven was uppermost in my mind. The dusk was descending as I arrived home, only to find my parents were not there.

Feeling lonely, I rummaged around in the buffet drawer for something to read. I found a pamphlet entitled "Heaven or Hell?" Dark was descending fast so I lit the kerosene lamp so I could read by the oil-cloth covered table.

The pamphlet mentioned some Bible verses in it and the first one was from *Romans 3:23. "For all have sinned and come short of the glory of God." I stopped a minute to think about that. I realized sin meant the bad things I had done, and it was certainly true of me.

Most of the time, I tried to mind my parents and do the right things, but there were moments! Whenever my girlfriend in school and I got mad, we pulled each other's hair so the older girls had to separate us.

Sometimes I would sneak off when it was time to do my chores and whenever I didn't want to be bothered with taking my little sister, Carol, to the outhouse. I told her there were ghosts in there! I had done wrong things all right!

I read more, *Romans 6:23: "For the wages (or payment) of that sin (or wrong doing) is death!" Oh, oh, I suppose that meant I would go to the other place than heaven and I sure didn't want to go there! The verse finished with "But the gift of God is eternal life!"

Going on I discovered *John 1:12: "But as many as received him, to them gave he the power to become the sons of God!" In other words, if I accepted him into my life, I could be sure of going to heaven some day.

There it was, the very answer I had been looking for these last nine years. Suddenly a light bulb clicked on in my head. I knelt down in the dimly-lit old farmhouse and simply asked Jesus to forgive me and come into my life. It felt as if a ton of worry was taken from me because now I knew for certain that I would go to heaven when I died. Not only that but I would see my sister, Luella, again!

Actually, I looked at the world through a different lens after that. Although I still had the normal everyday problems of life, I felt so good knowing I had someone who would help me with all my life decisions, as well as the problems of everyday living.

And I can truthfully say God has directed my life. Not that I was always in fellowship with him. Sometimes, like a daughter, I had to learn the hard way. He did, however, lead me to make the right friends, marry the right man, teach me things in being a mother, and give me the joy of writing.

Accepting Christ as my own was the biggest and most important decision of my life!

* **KJV** Bible

Chapter 35

Farewell to the Country School

Sunrise School students that attended while we were in California: Teacher: Amelia Mueller, Roland Reimer, Vernon Thiessen, Delmer Reimer, unknown, Frank Thiessen. Second row: Evelyn Friesen, Rosella Friesen, Verna Unruh, Velma Gaeddert, Meribeth Thiessen. Front row: Ervin Unruh, Harvey Thiessen & Ruth Friesen

The world is changing at an even faster rate than has ever been recorded in history. I am sorry to see some things go into oblivion because they had special meaning to many of us. One of those things was the little country school that dotted the country in the thirties and forties. Both my parents had taught in them in earlier days and had told me many exciting stories about some of their episodes. The days we lived on the farm gave me some special days to enjoy in the little one room school of Sunrise, District 160.

The special year I am talking about was in the forties. We had moved around a lot in my younger grade school years, Oklahoma, Texas, Dodge City, three places in Hutchinson, the farm, four places in California and then back to the farm I was used to change but this one seemed to be more hurtful. I had really bonded to the country school. Now, my grandparents had sold the farm and we would be moving to Hutch again. This time it was more bittersweet and obviously I was not looking forward to the change.

The whole earth was blossoming with spring. Fields were turning green with the lush growth of emerald wheat and I, as a twelve-year-old, eagerly looked forward to the mile walk to school down the country road. The cheery robins and even the old crows in the shelterbelt voiced their melody in the crisp, country air and one couldn't help but feel the renewing of life that this season brings.

Still, I felt heart heavy. The twelve students and the teacher had become familiar and I knew I would miss the family atmosphere we enjoyed in the country.

I could remember so many happy times, the basketball games we played on the grass outside court, the spelling contests, the camaraderie we felt with our classmates of eight grades.

This year, the teacher had asked me to sing a solo, my very first, in public. We practiced for our Last Day of School Program, which came at the end of April.

The parents all came to the school and we gave our little program, a few musical numbers and pieces with the help of the big roll-down curtain in the front. the audience didn't mind waiting a little between numbers because they could read all the advertisements from the surrounding areas, The Buhler State Bank, Lindas Lumber Company, the Nyal Store and of course, the Food Market.

Finally, it was time for my solo. The butterflies in my stomach turned somersaults and I can remember thinking to myself "You actually wanted to do this?" I stood in the front by the piano and felt my knees begin to shake. Then I looked at the audience of parents, and especially my own mom. She was smiling and nodding her head slightly and I knew I could do it. The song "Farewell to Thee" was sung with all the feeling I had been hoarding: "Now our golden days are at an end, the parting hour will be here soon. And we think as swift the moments fly. How delightful has been our friendship's boon." Afterwards, I remember thinking, "How strange, I actually enjoyed singing!"

After the program, everyone piled into their vehicles and we drove to a nearby pasture located near the Little Arkansas River. The men put pieces of plywood on wooden sawhorses and the women laid out the cloths and the food: fried chicken, potato salad, pies, bread, cake and beans.

We older kids sat down on some logs by the river and talked about what we would do some day. We played

"Johnny can't cross my river" and enjoyed ourselves as kids one more time.

Then we heard our parents call "Come and eat!" and we all ran with one accord to the food-laden tables. The school board had even purchased some ice cream bars that were packed in dry ice and we thought our lives had reached the ultimate level of luxury.

All too soon, our parents started calling us that it was time to go home. I could feel the bitter sweetness of the day. After harvest my family would be moving back to Hutch and I would no longer feel the camaraderie of the kids at Sunrise.

It was only a few years later, the district consolidated the schools and Sunrise was moved away to an unknown destination.

I wish everyone could have a chance to enjoy life in the country as it was back then for at least a part of their lives. But now, even the presidential candidates say "We need change!" But do we really?

Although we have had to say farewell to the country school, I will never forget the lessons God taught me within her boundaries. It was the "sunrise of my learning about life, and even more important, about God."

Sunrise School will always have a special place in my treasure box of memories!

Remember When

Printed in the United States
204637BV00003B/244-330/P